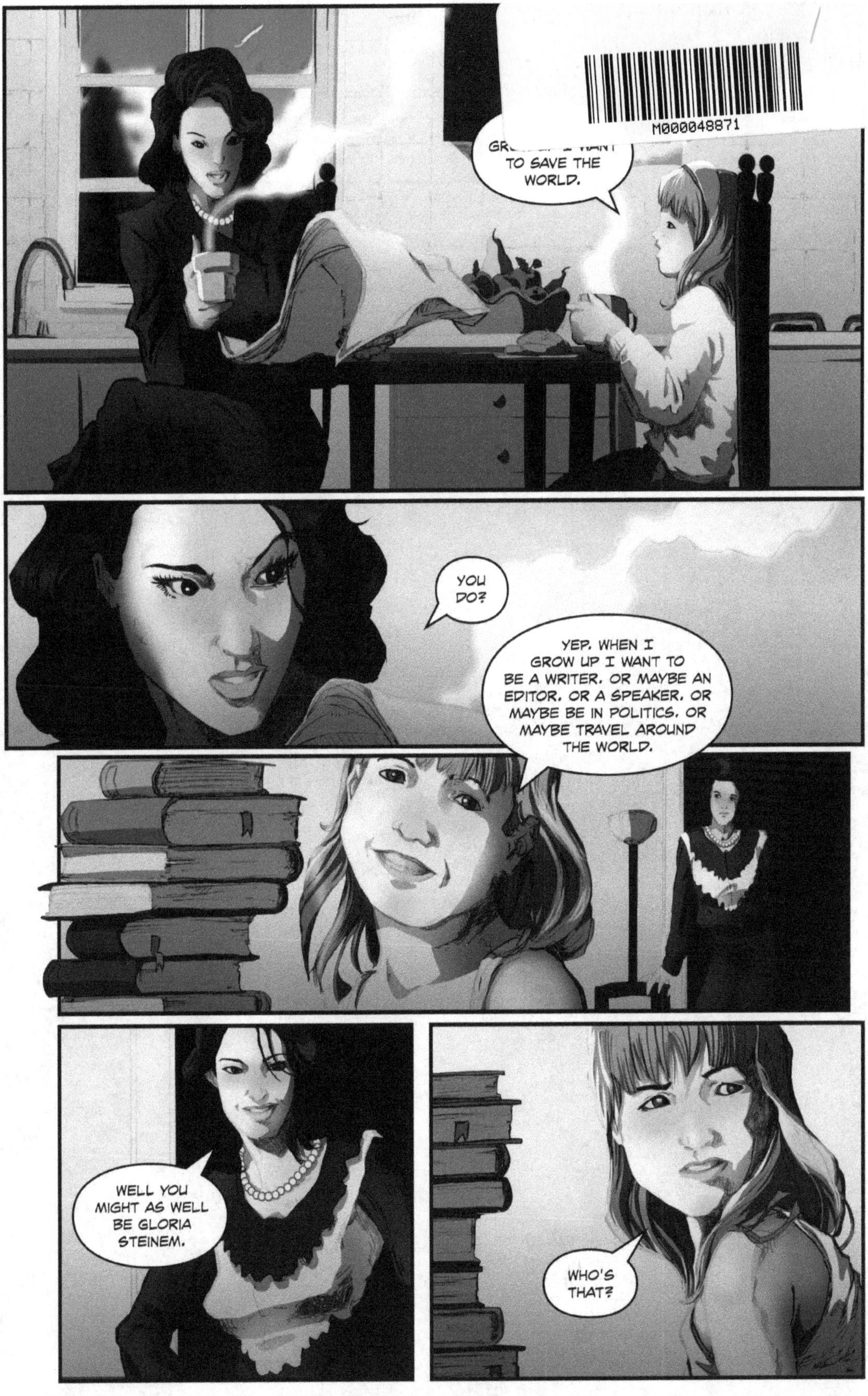

TO SAVE THE WORLD.
YOU DO?
YEP. WHEN I GROW UP I WANT TO BE A WRITER. OR MAYBE AN EDITOR. OR A SPEAKER. OR MAYBE BE IN POLITICS. OR MAYBE TRAVEL AROUND THE WORLD.
WELL YOU MIGHT AS WELL BE GLORIA STEINEM.
WHO'S THAT?

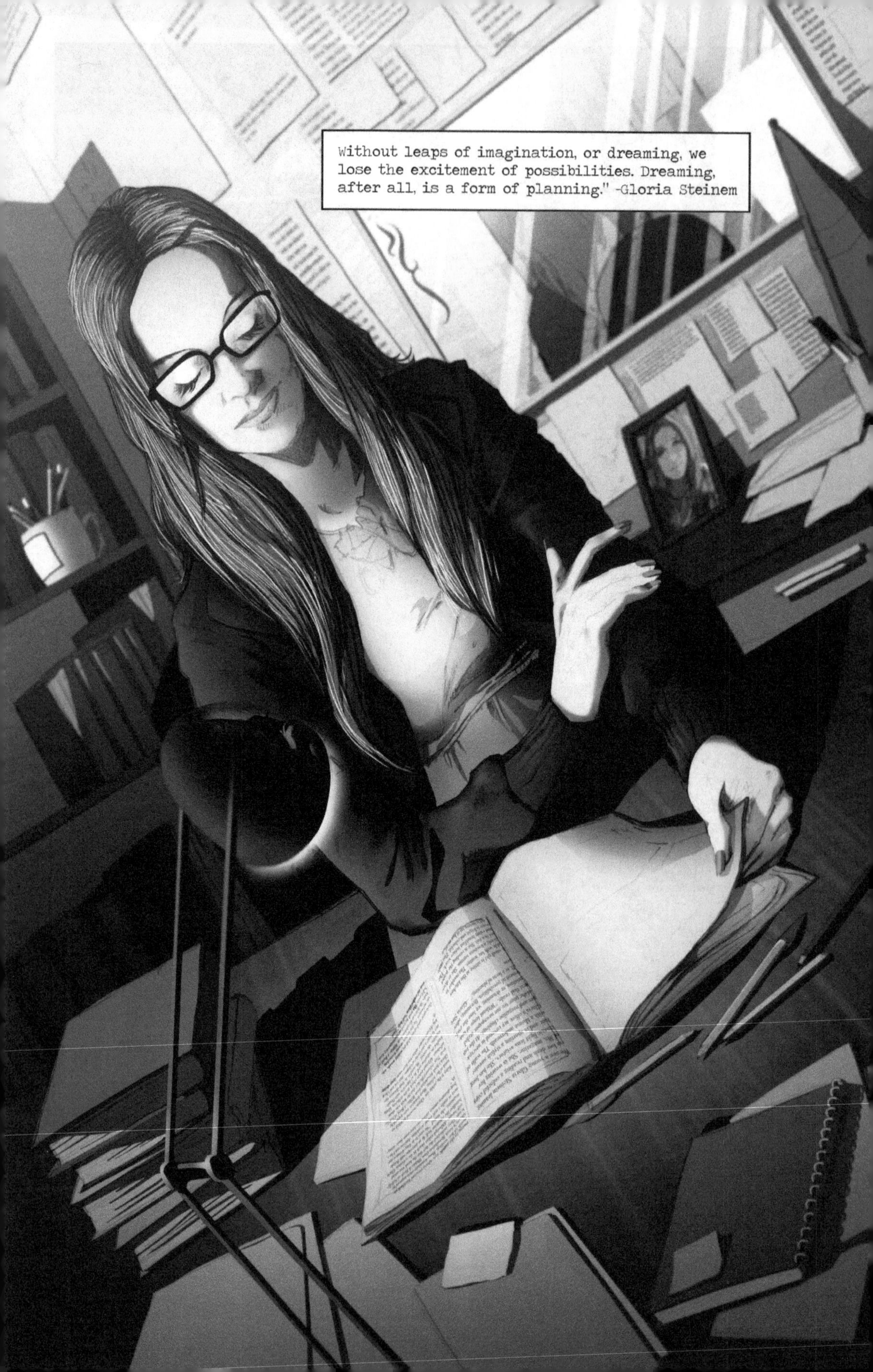
Without leaps of imagination, or dreaming, we lose the excitement of possibilities. Dreaming, after all, is a form of planning." -Gloria Steinem

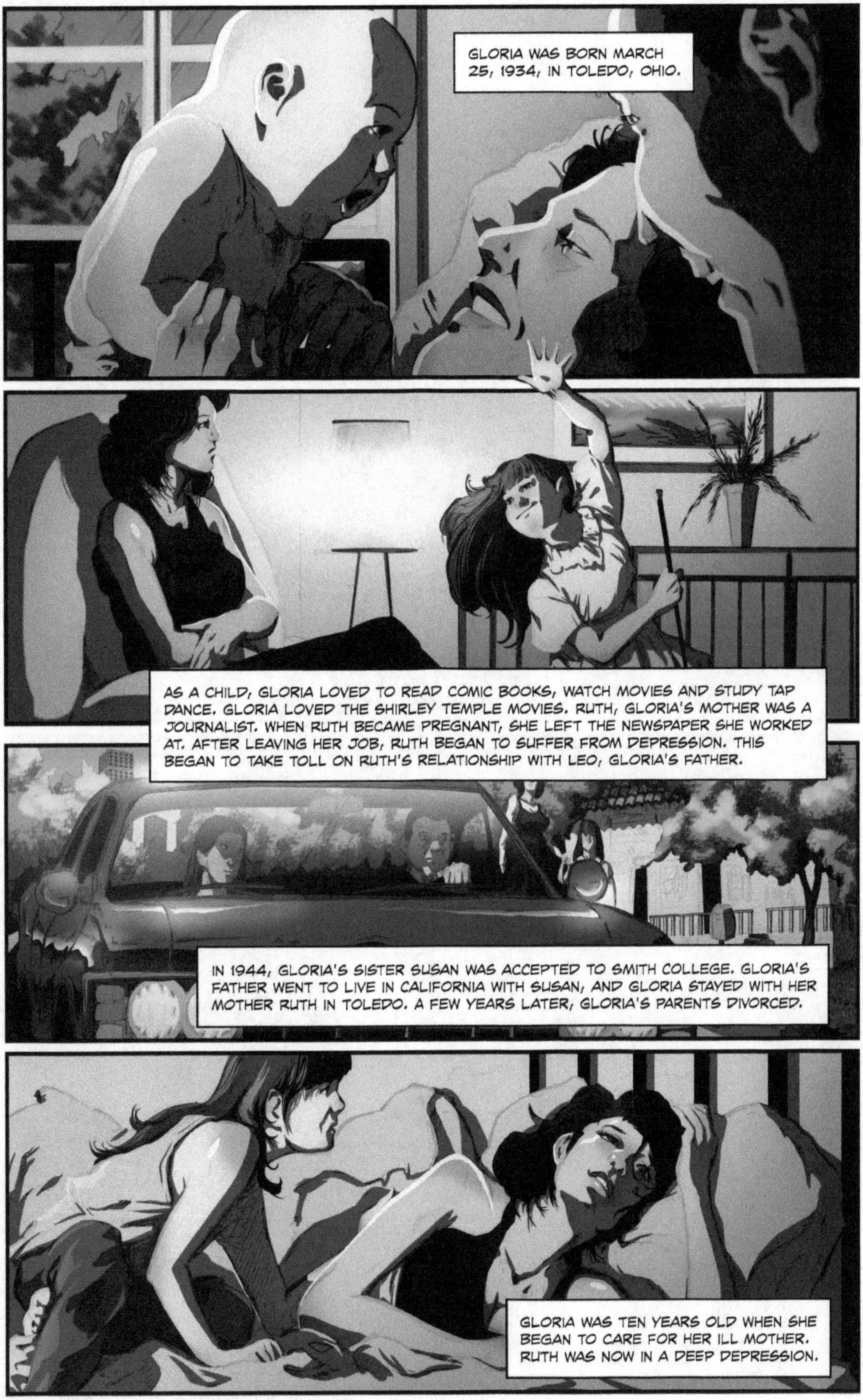
GLORIA WAS BORN MARCH 25, 1934, IN TOLEDO, OHIO.
AS A CHILD, GLORIA LOVED TO READ COMIC BOOKS, WATCH MOVIES AND STUDY TAP DANCE. GLORIA LOVED THE SHIRLEY TEMPLE MOVIES. RUTH, GLORIA'S MOTHER WAS A JOURNALIST. WHEN RUTH BECAME PREGNANT, SHE LEFT THE NEWSPAPER SHE WORKED AT. AFTER LEAVING HER JOB, RUTH BEGAN TO SUFFER FROM DEPRESSION. THIS BEGAN TO TAKE TOLL ON RUTH'S RELATIONSHIP WITH LEO, GLORIA'S FATHER.
IN 1944, GLORIA'S SISTER SUSAN WAS ACCEPTED TO SMITH COLLEGE. GLORIA'S FATHER WENT TO LIVE IN CALIFORNIA WITH SUSAN, AND GLORIA STAYED WITH HER MOTHER RUTH IN TOLEDO. A FEW YEARS LATER, GLORIA'S PARENTS DIVORCED.
GLORIA WAS TEN YEARS OLD WHEN SHE BEGAN TO CARE FOR HER ILL MOTHER. RUTH WAS NOW IN A DEEP DEPRESSION.

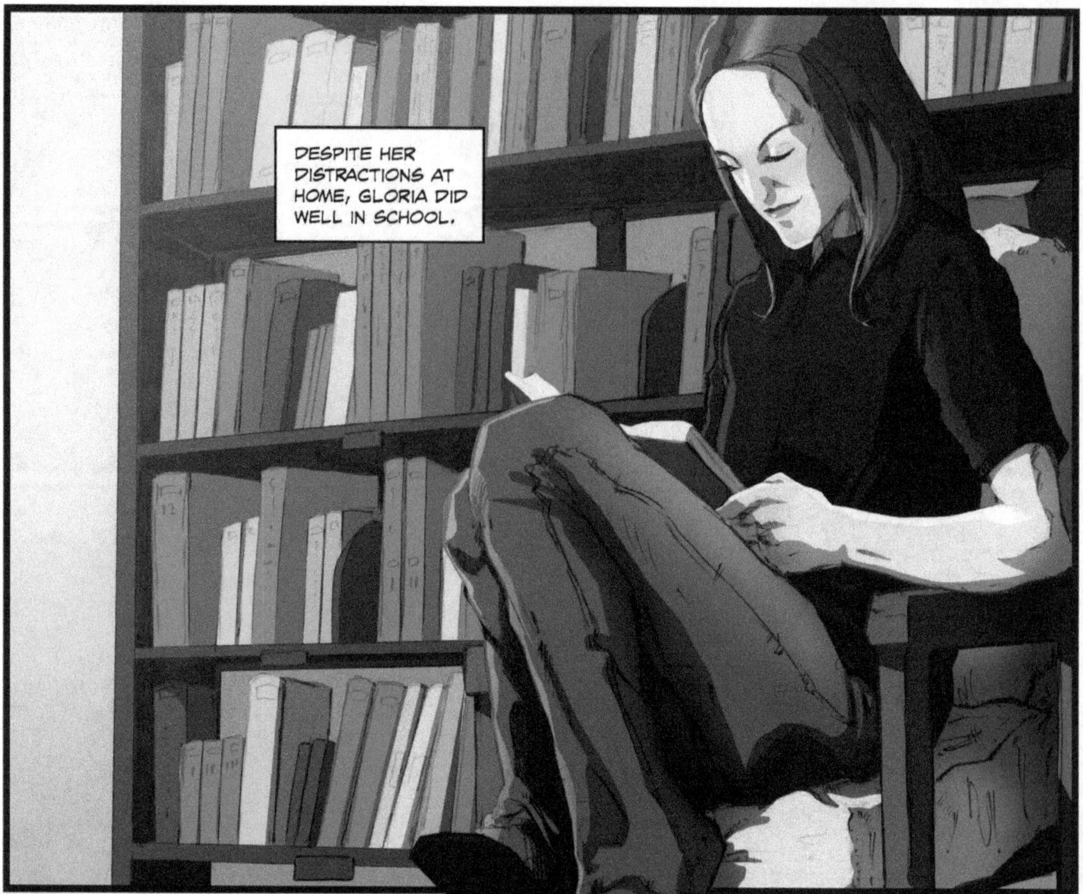
DESPITE HER DISTRACTIONS AT HOME, GLORIA DID WELL IN SCHOOL.

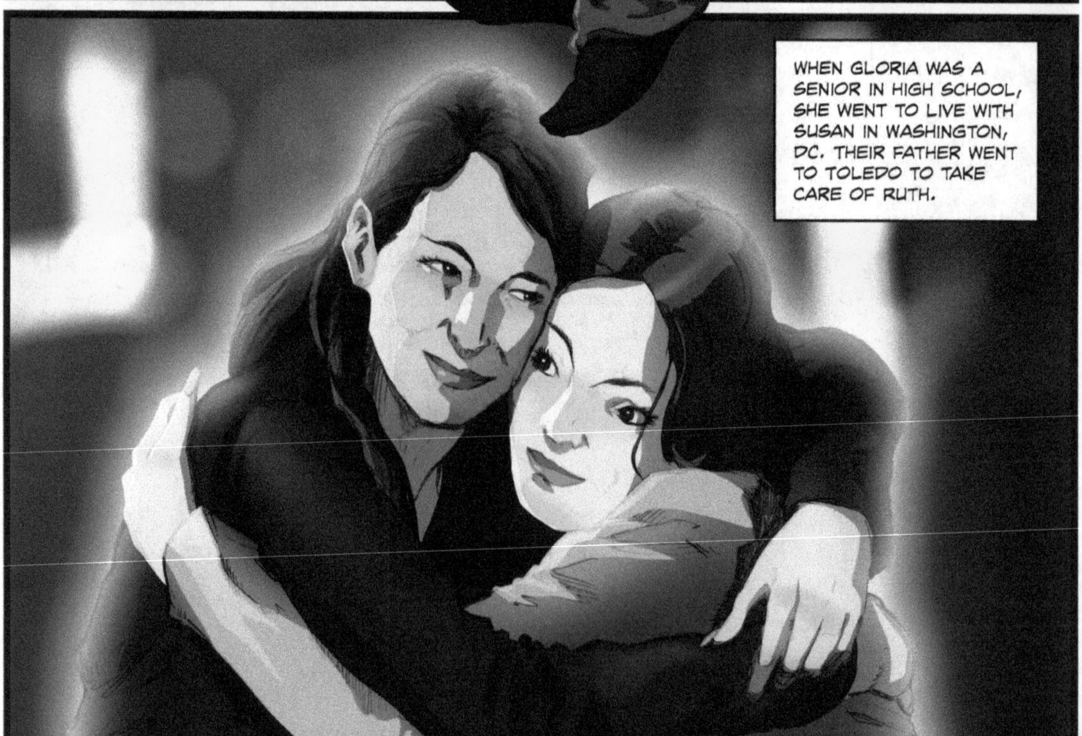
WHEN GLORIA WAS A SENIOR IN HIGH SCHOOL, SHE WENT TO LIVE WITH SUSAN IN WASHINGTON, DC. THEIR FATHER WENT TO TOLEDO TO TAKE CARE OF RUTH.

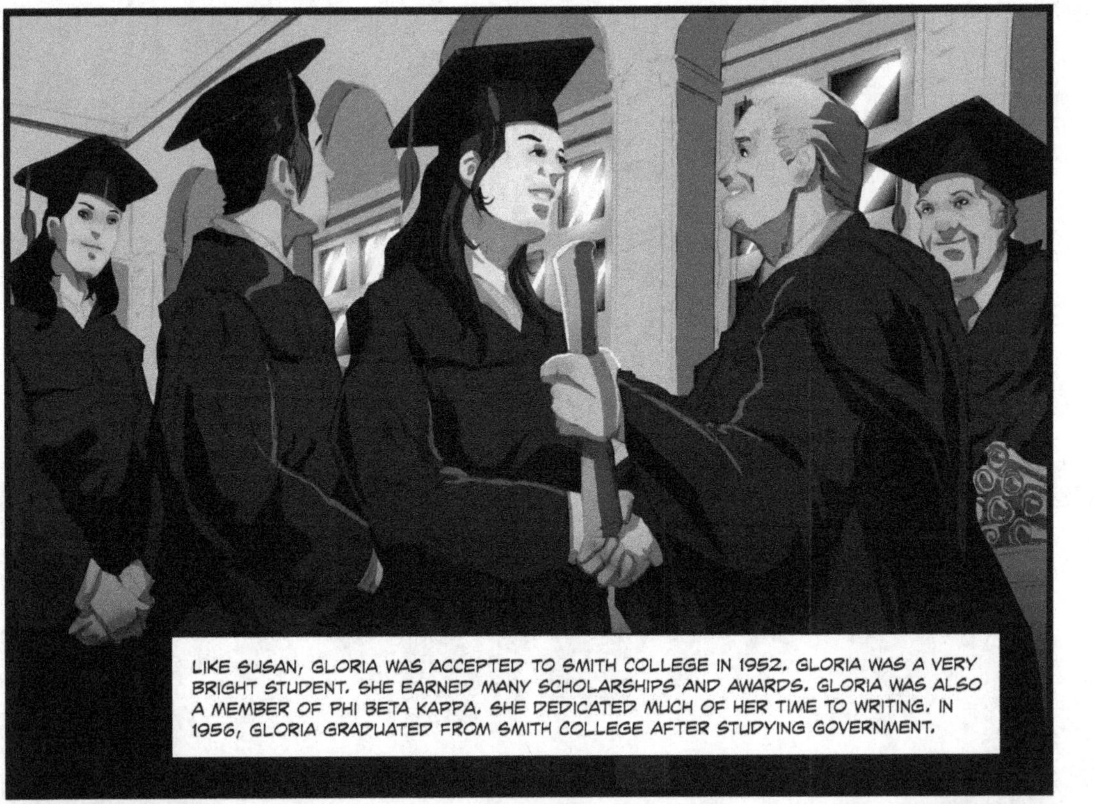
LIKE SUSAN, GLORIA WAS ACCEPTED TO SMITH COLLEGE IN 1952. GLORIA WAS A VERY BRIGHT STUDENT. SHE EARNED MANY SCHOLARSHIPS AND AWARDS. GLORIA WAS ALSO A MEMBER OF PHI BETA KAPPA. SHE DEDICATED MUCH OF HER TIME TO WRITING. IN 1956, GLORIA GRADUATED FROM SMITH COLLEGE AFTER STUDYING GOVERNMENT.

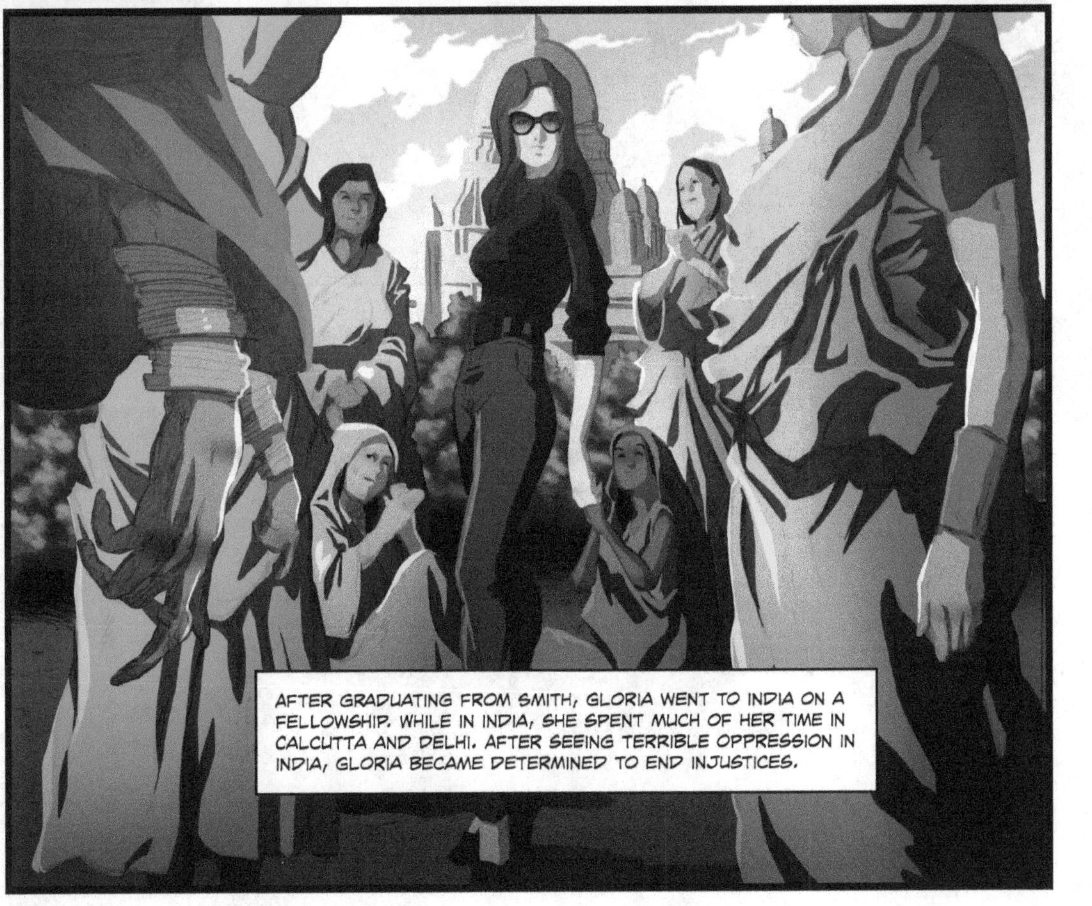
AFTER GRADUATING FROM SMITH, GLORIA WENT TO INDIA ON A FELLOWSHIP. WHILE IN INDIA, SHE SPENT MUCH OF HER TIME IN CALCUTTA AND DELHI. AFTER SEEING TERRIBLE OPPRESSION IN INDIA, GLORIA BECAME DETERMINED TO END INJUSTICES.

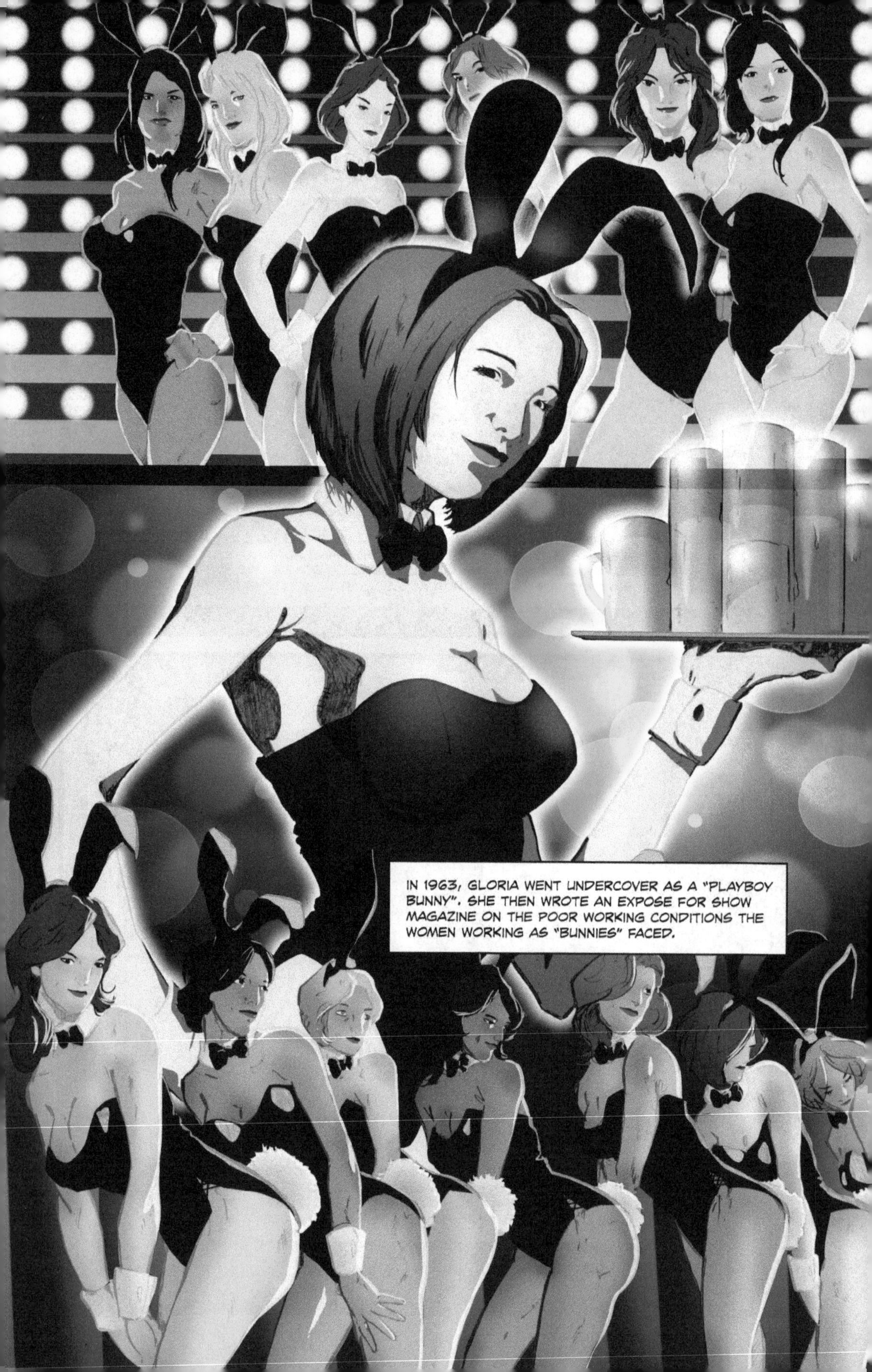
IN 1963, GLORIA WENT UNDERCOVER AS A "PLAYBOY BUNNY". SHE THEN WROTE AN EXPOSE FOR SHOW MAGAZINE ON THE POOR WORKING CONDITIONS THE WOMEN WORKING AS "BUNNIES" FACED.

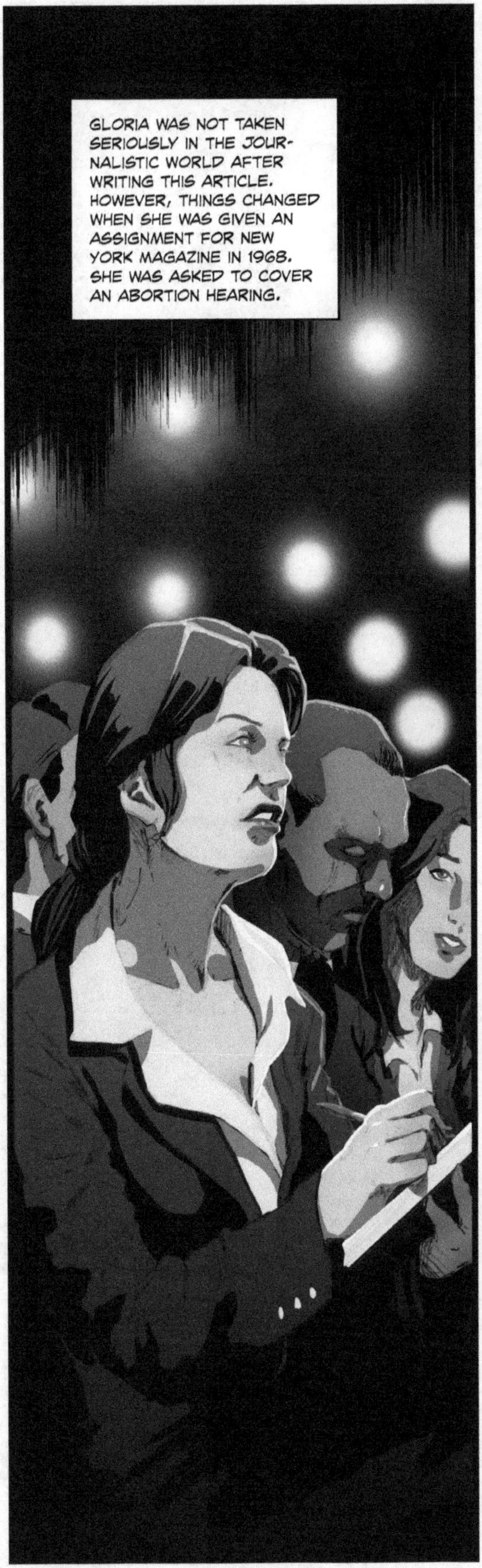
GLORIA WAS NOT TAKEN SERIOUSLY IN THE JOURNALISTIC WORLD AFTER WRITING THIS ARTICLE. HOWEVER, THINGS CHANGED WHEN SHE WAS GIVEN AN ASSIGNMENT FOR NEW YORK MAGAZINE IN 1968. SHE WAS ASKED TO COVER AN ABORTION HEARING.

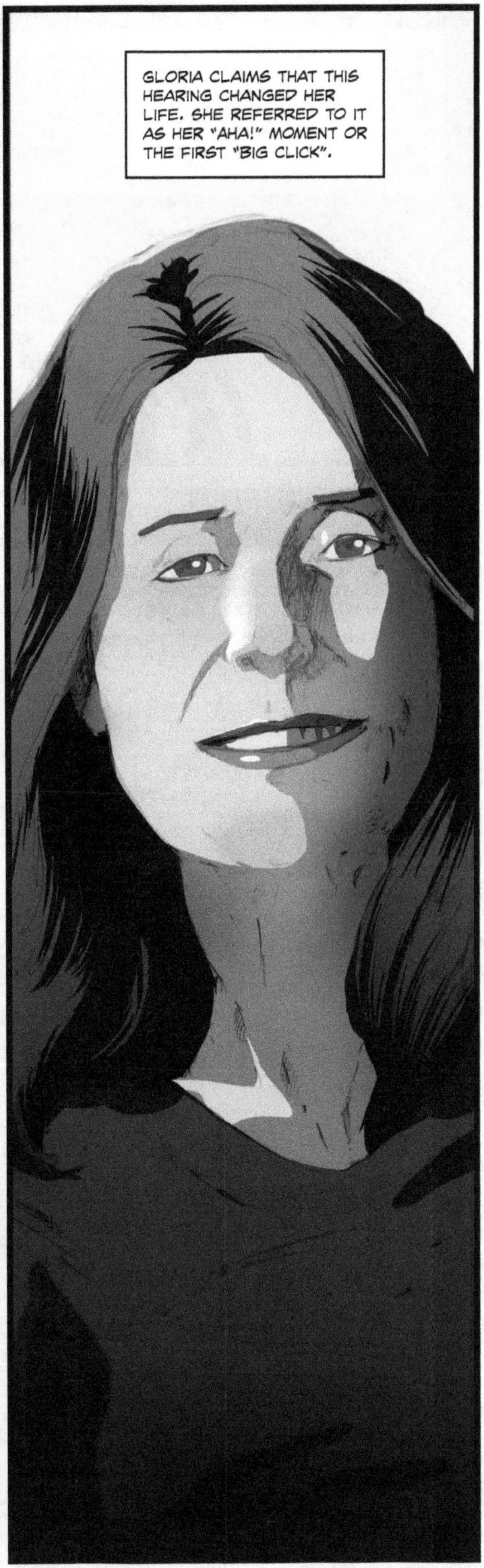
GLORIA CLAIMS THAT THIS HEARING CHANGED HER LIFE. SHE REFERRED TO IT AS HER "AHA!" MOMENT OR THE FIRST "BIG CLICK".

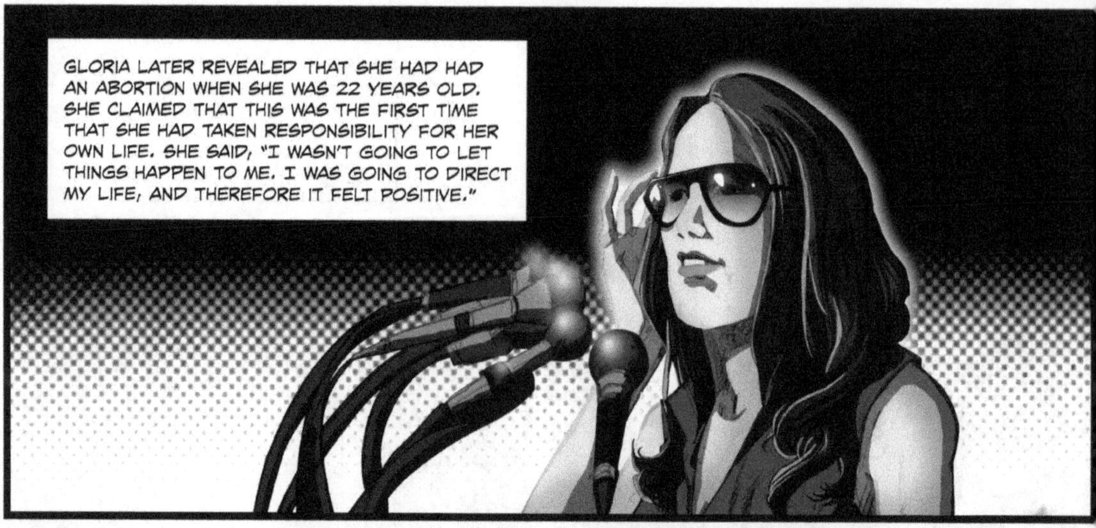
GLORIA LATER REVEALED THAT SHE HAD HAD AN ABORTION WHEN SHE WAS 22 YEARS OLD. SHE CLAIMED THAT THIS WAS THE FIRST TIME THAT SHE HAD TAKEN RESPONSIBILITY FOR HER OWN LIFE. SHE SAID, "I WASN'T GOING TO LET THINGS HAPPEN TO ME. I WAS GOING TO DIRECT MY LIFE, AND THEREFORE IT FELT POSITIVE."

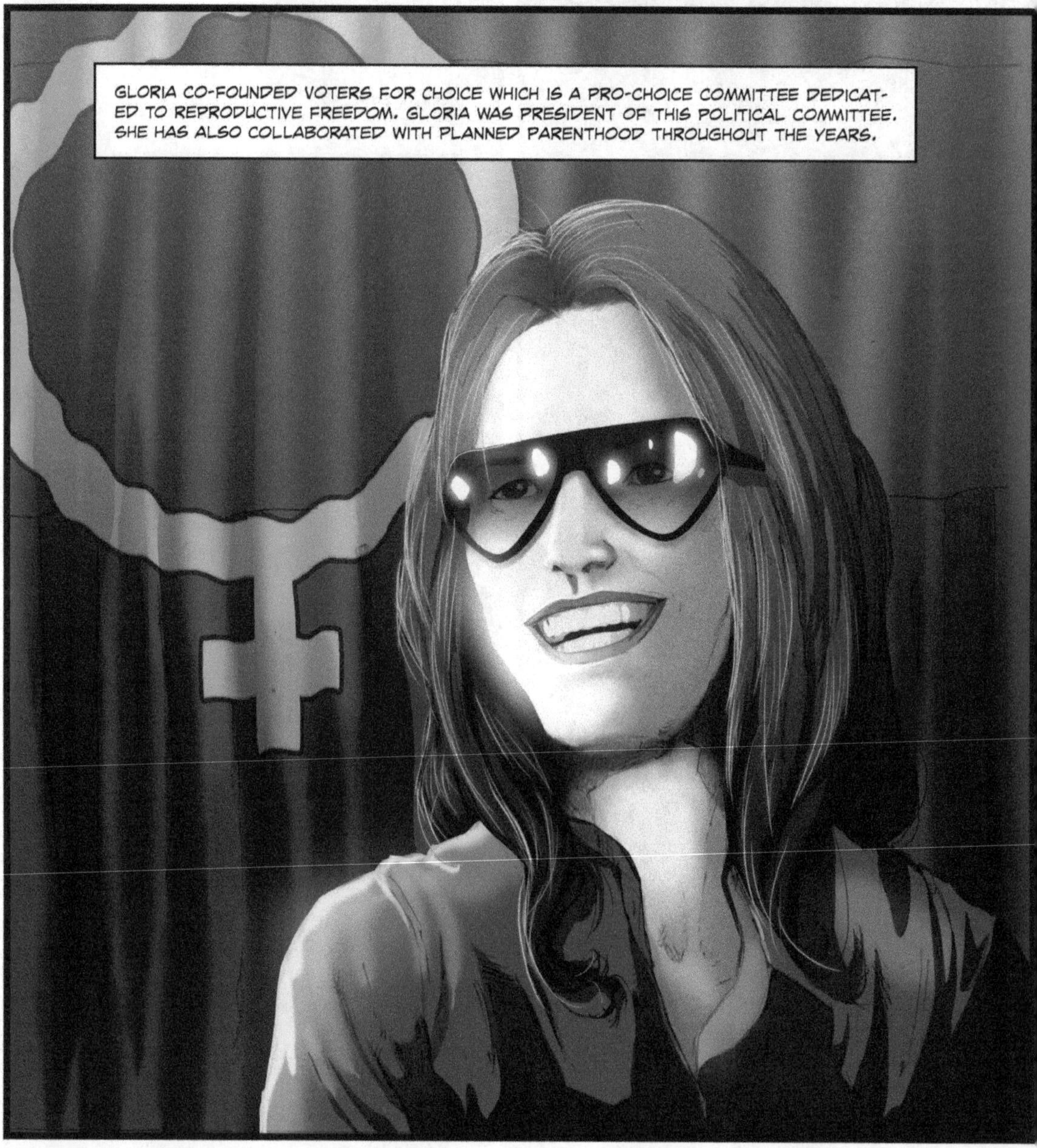
GLORIA CO-FOUNDED VOTERS FOR CHOICE WHICH IS A PRO-CHOICE COMMITTEE DEDICATED TO REPRODUCTIVE FREEDOM. GLORIA WAS PRESIDENT OF THIS POLITICAL COMMITTEE. SHE HAS ALSO COLLABORATED WITH PLANNED PARENTHOOD THROUGHOUT THE YEARS.

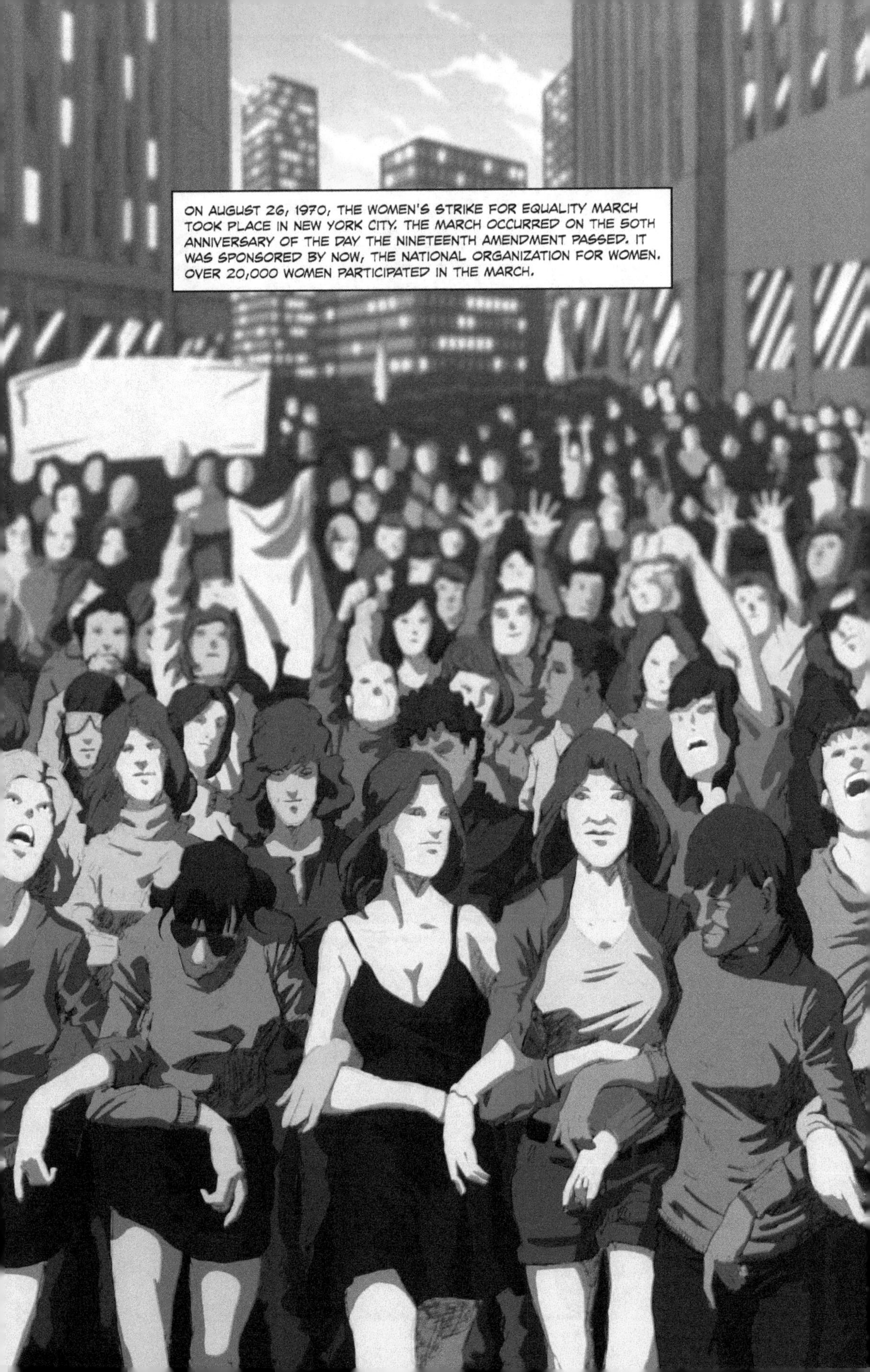
ON AUGUST 26, 1970, THE WOMEN'S STRIKE FOR EQUALITY MARCH TOOK PLACE IN NEW YORK CITY. THE MARCH OCCURRED ON THE 50TH ANNIVERSARY OF THE DAY THE NINETEENTH AMENDMENT PASSED. IT WAS SPONSORED BY NOW, THE NATIONAL ORGANIZATION FOR WOMEN. OVER 20,000 WOMEN PARTICIPATED IN THE MARCH.

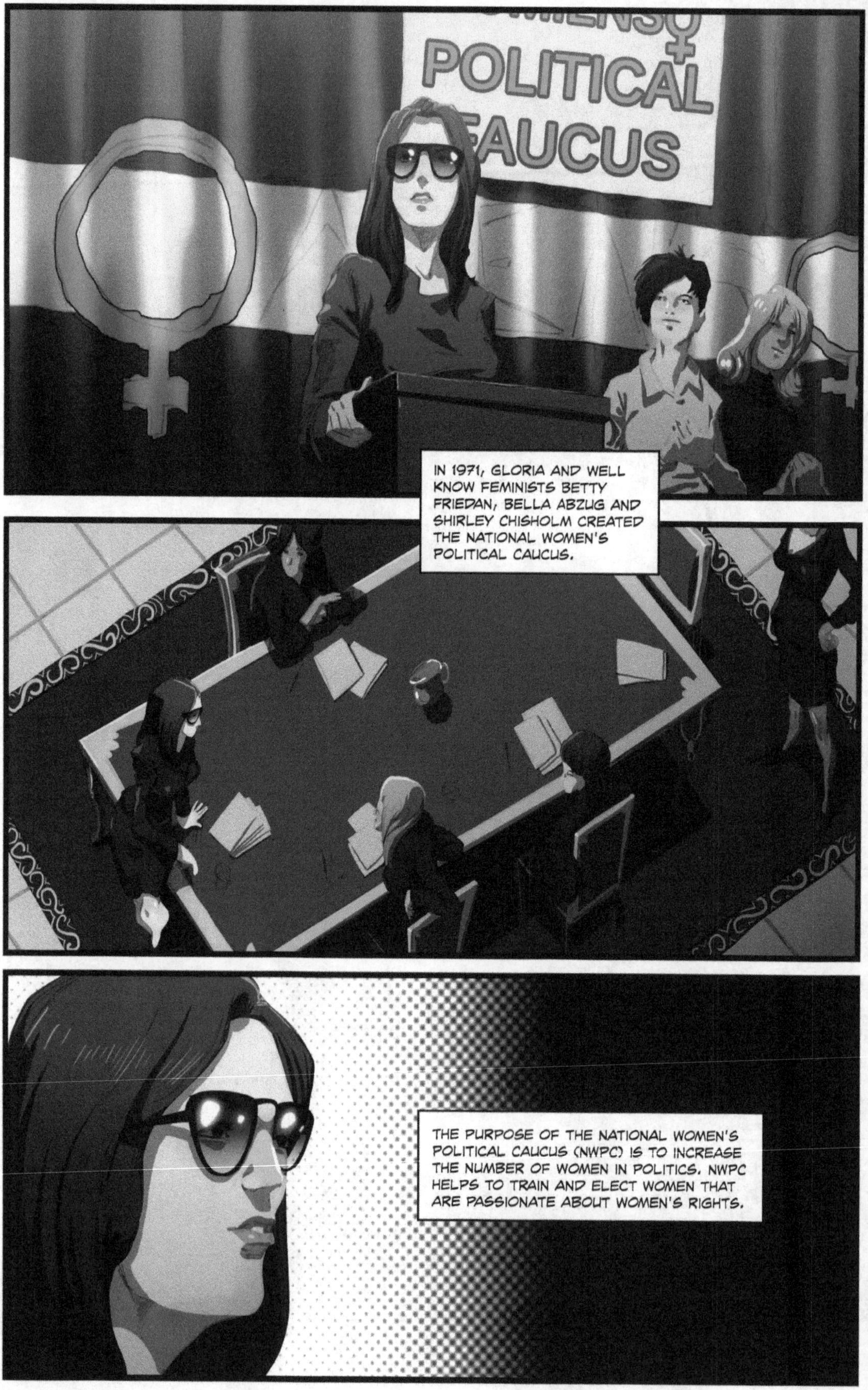
POLITICAL
IN 1971, GLORIA AND WELL KNOW FEMINISTS BETTY FRIEDAN, BELLA ABZUG AND SHIRLEY CHISHOLM CREATED THE NATIONAL WOMEN'S POLITICAL CAUCUS.
THE PURPOSE OF THE NATIONAL WOMEN'S POLITICAL CAUCUS (NWPC) IS TO INCREASE THE NUMBER OF WOMEN IN POLITICS. NWPC HELPS TO TRAIN AND ELECT WOMEN THAT ARE PASSIONATE ABOUT WOMEN'S RIGHTS.

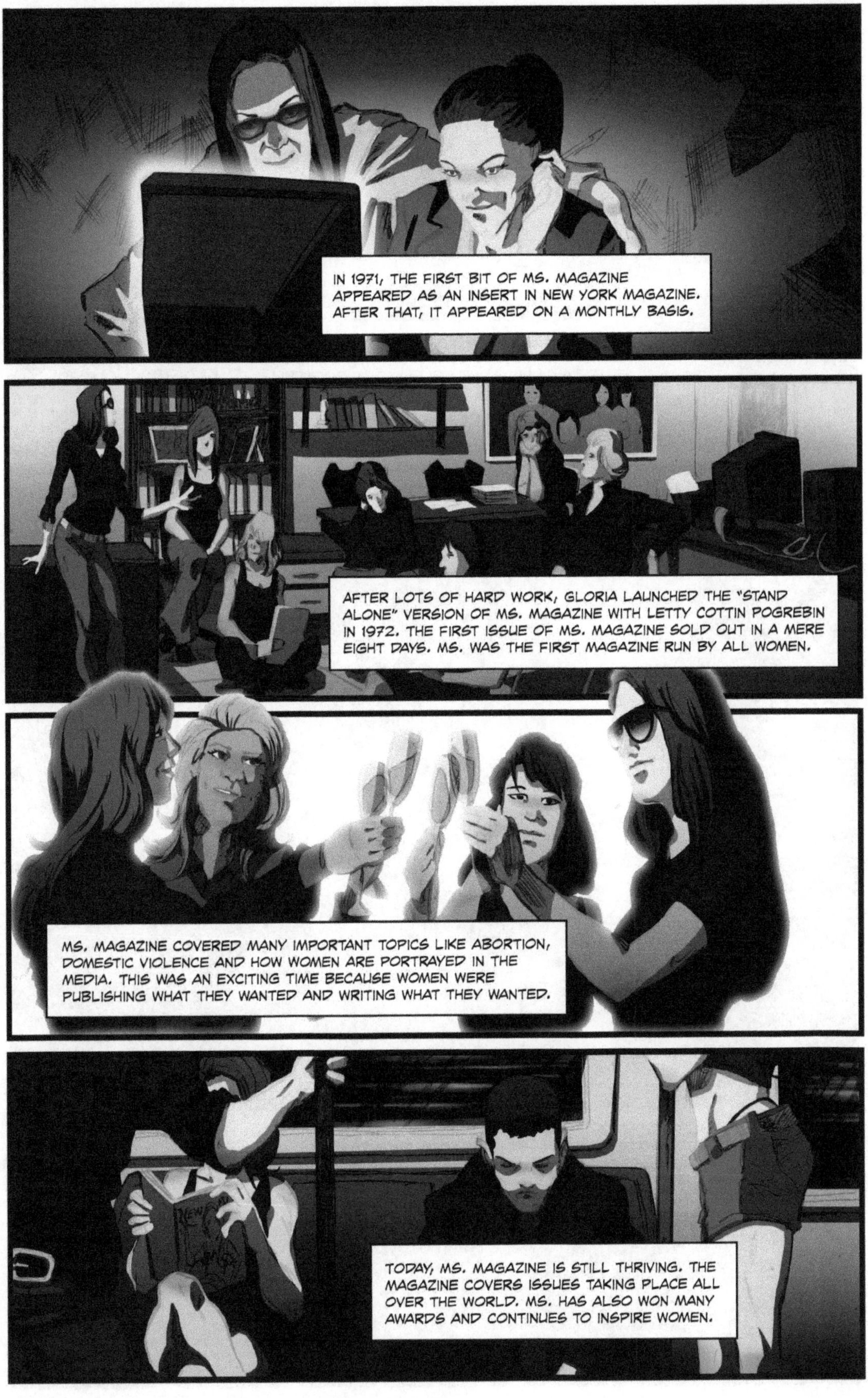
IN 1971, THE FIRST BIT OF MS. MAGAZINE APPEARED AS AN INSERT IN NEW YORK MAGAZINE. AFTER THAT, IT APPEARED ON A MONTHLY BASIS.
AFTER LOTS OF HARD WORK, GLORIA LAUNCHED THE "STAND ALONE" VERSION OF MS. MAGAZINE WITH LETTY COTTIN POGREBIN IN 1972. THE FIRST ISSUE OF MS. MAGAZINE SOLD OUT IN A MERE EIGHT DAYS. MS. WAS THE FIRST MAGAZINE RUN BY ALL WOMEN.
MS. MAGAZINE COVERED MANY IMPORTANT TOPICS LIKE ABORTION, DOMESTIC VIOLENCE AND HOW WOMEN ARE PORTRAYED IN THE MEDIA. THIS WAS AN EXCITING TIME BECAUSE WOMEN WERE PUBLISHING WHAT THEY WANTED AND WRITING WHAT THEY WANTED.
TODAY, MS. MAGAZINE IS STILL THRIVING. THE MAGAZINE COVERS ISSUES TAKING PLACE ALL OVER THE WORLD. MS. HAS ALSO WON MANY AWARDS AND CONTINUES TO INSPIRE WOMEN.

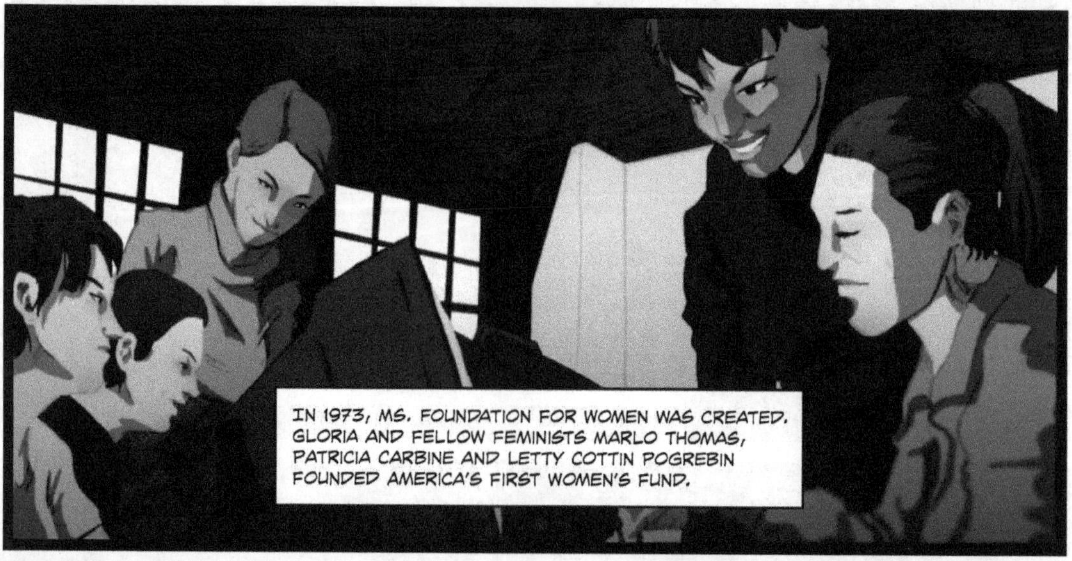
IN 1973, MS. FOUNDATION FOR WOMEN WAS CREATED. GLORIA AND FELLOW FEMINISTS MARLO THOMAS, PATRICIA CARBINE AND LETTY COTTIN POGREBIN FOUNDED AMERICA'S FIRST WOMEN'S FUND.

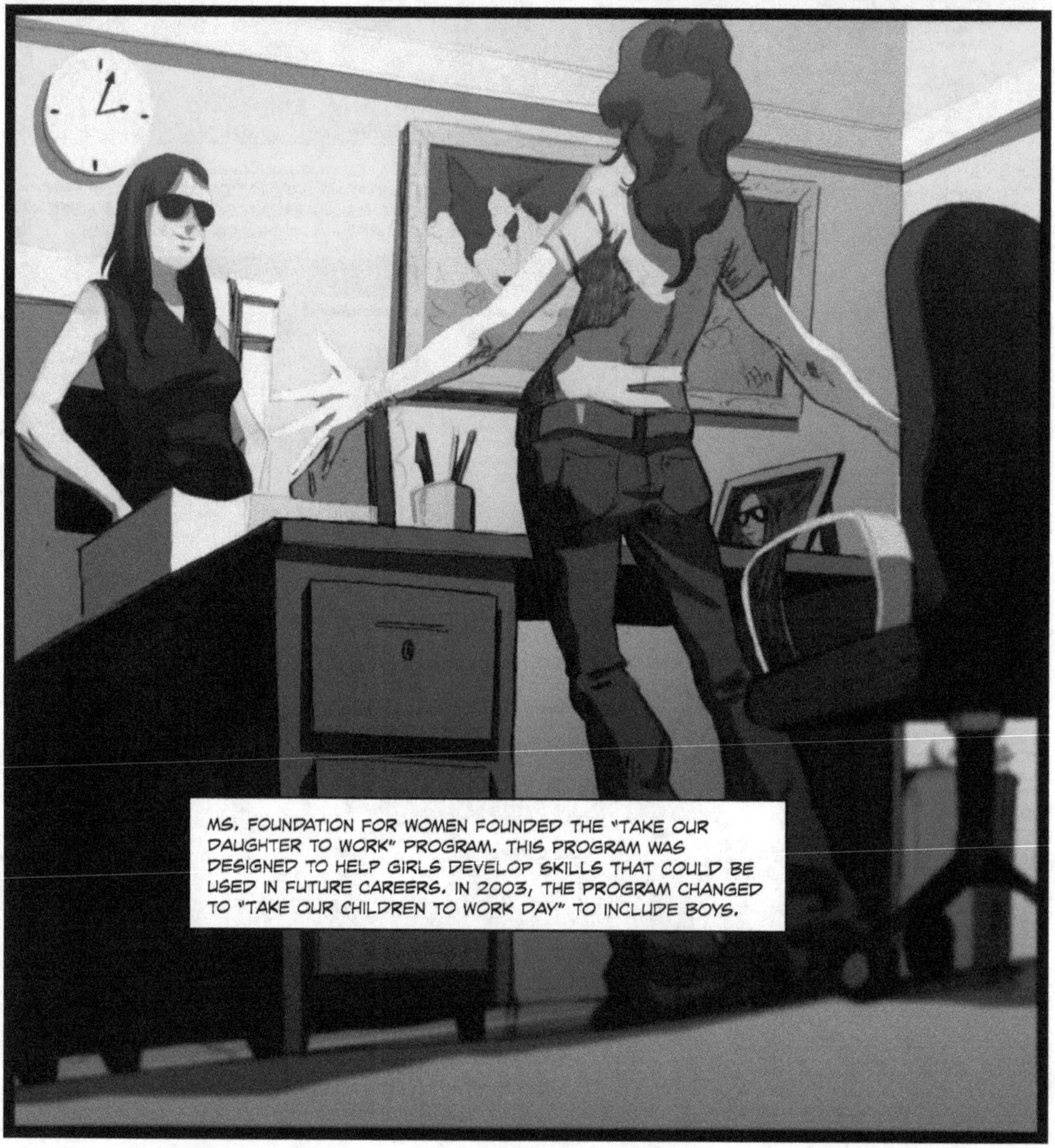
MS. FOUNDATION FOR WOMEN FOUNDED THE "TAKE OUR DAUGHTER TO WORK" PROGRAM. THIS PROGRAM WAS DESIGNED TO HELP GIRLS DEVELOP SKILLS THAT COULD BE USED IN FUTURE CAREERS. IN 2003, THE PROGRAM CHANGED TO "TAKE OUR CHILDREN TO WORK DAY" TO INCLUDE BOYS.

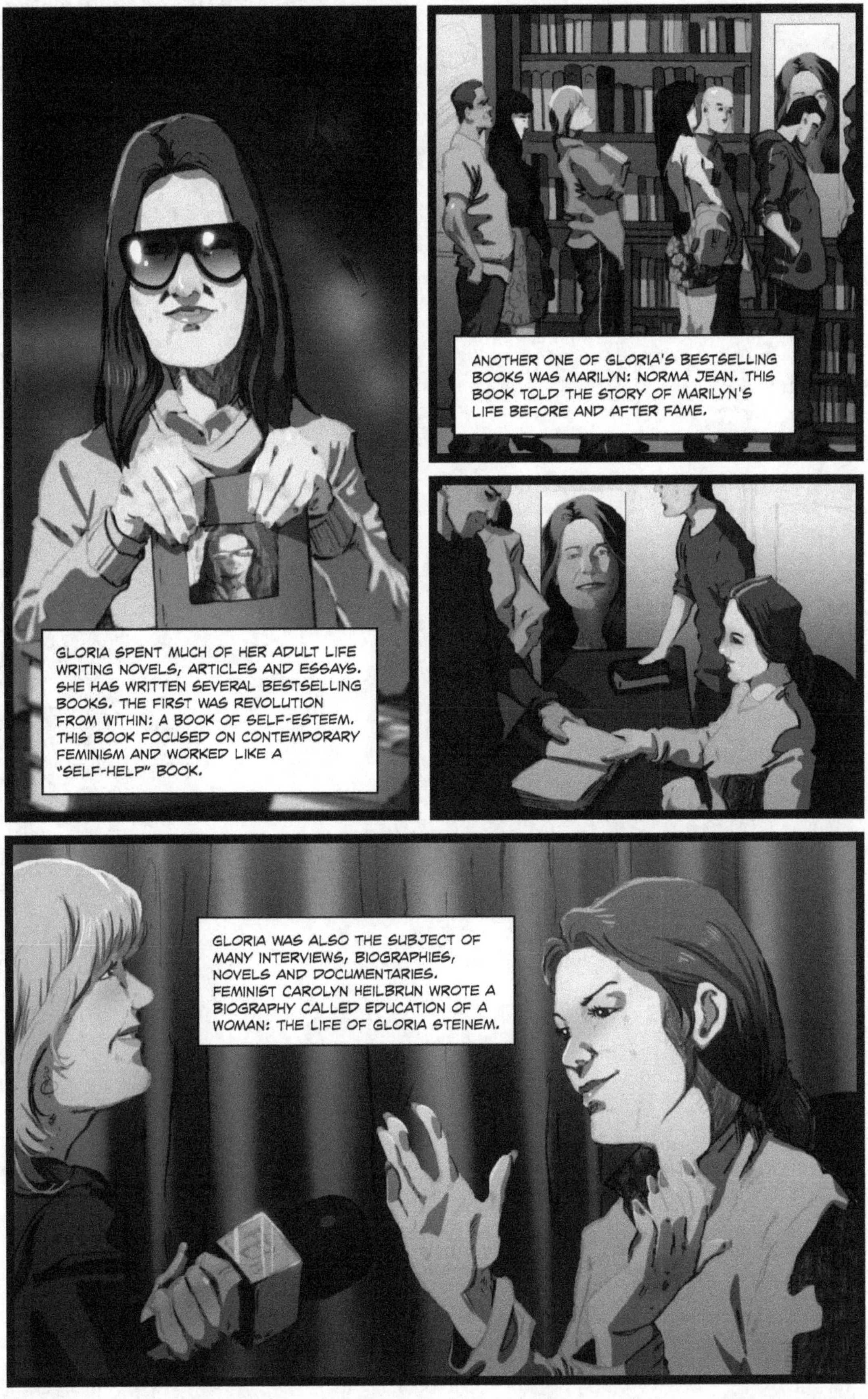
GLORIA SPENT MUCH OF HER ADULT LIFE WRITING NOVELS, ARTICLES AND ESSAYS. SHE HAS WRITTEN SEVERAL BESTSELLING BOOKS. THE FIRST WAS REVOLUTION FROM WITHIN: A BOOK OF SELF-ESTEEM. THIS BOOK FOCUSED ON CONTEMPORARY FEMINISM AND WORKED LIKE A "SELF-HELP" BOOK.
ANOTHER ONE OF GLORIA'S BESTSELLING BOOKS WAS MARILYN: NORMA JEAN. THIS BOOK TOLD THE STORY OF MARILYN'S LIFE BEFORE AND AFTER FAME.
GLORIA WAS ALSO THE SUBJECT OF MANY INTERVIEWS, BIOGRAPHIES, NOVELS AND DOCUMENTARIES. FEMINIST CAROLYN HEILBRUN WROTE A BIOGRAPHY CALLED EDUCATION OF A WOMAN: THE LIFE OF GLORIA STEINEM.

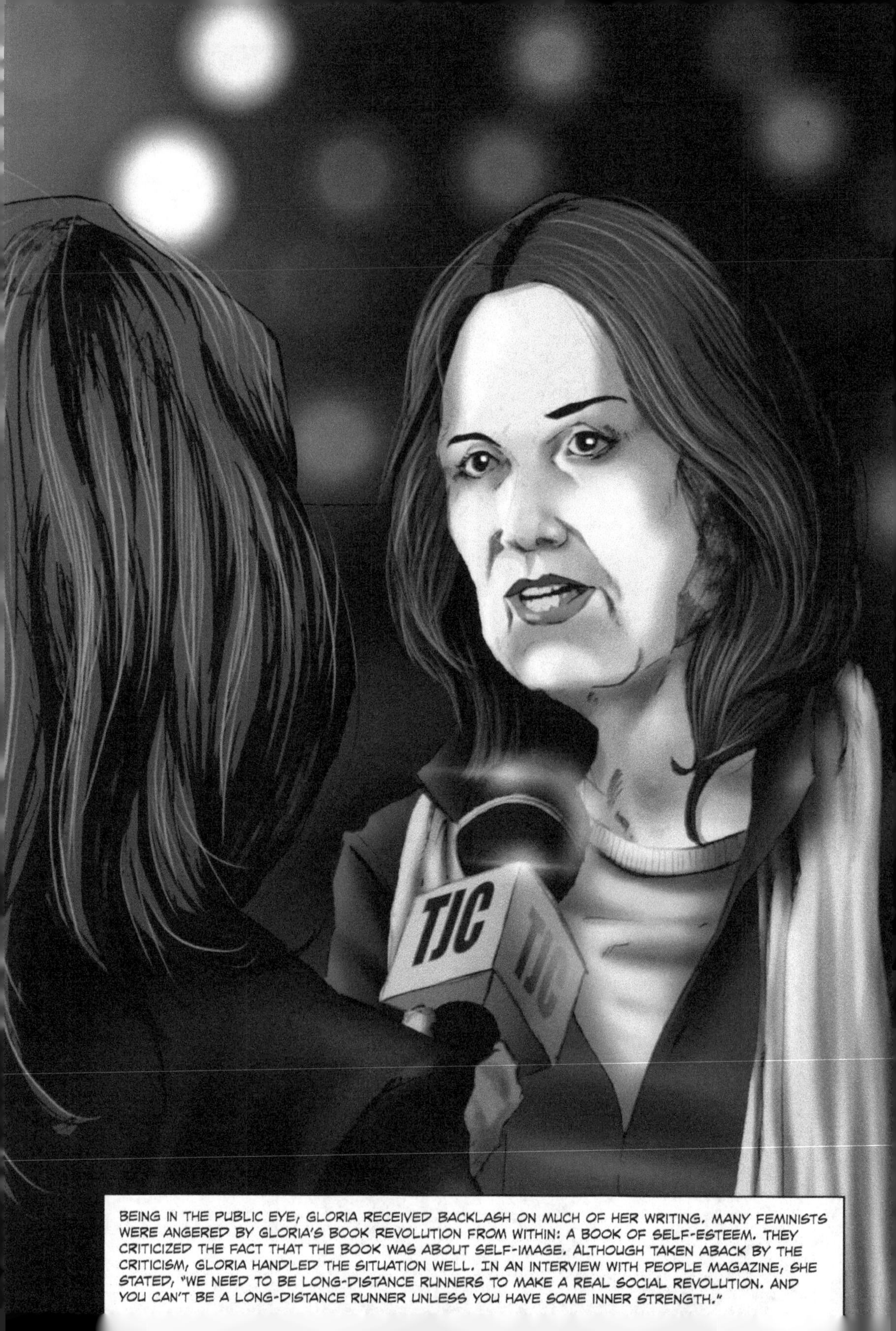
TJC
BEING IN THE PUBLIC EYE, GLORIA RECEIVED BACKLASH ON MUCH OF HER WRITING. MANY FEMINISTS WERE ANGERED BY GLORIA'S BOOK REVOLUTION FROM WITHIN: A BOOK OF SELF-ESTEEM. THEY CRITICIZED THE FACT THAT THE BOOK WAS ABOUT SELF-IMAGE. ALTHOUGH TAKEN ABACK BY THE CRITICISM, GLORIA HANDLED THE SITUATION WELL. IN AN INTERVIEW WITH PEOPLE MAGAZINE, SHE STATED, "WE NEED TO BE LONG-DISTANCE RUNNERS TO MAKE A REAL SOCIAL REVOLUTION. AND YOU CAN'T BE A LONG-DISTANCE RUNNER UNLESS YOU HAVE SOME INNER STRENGTH."

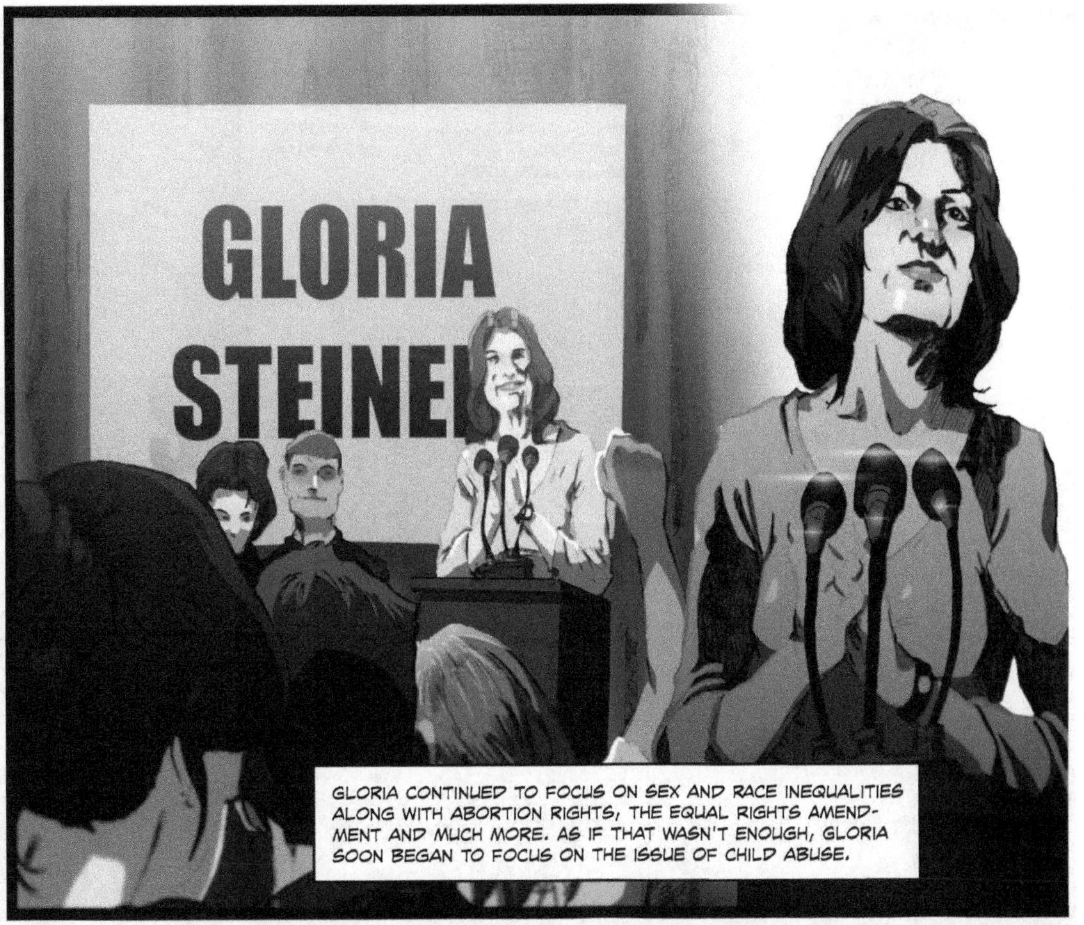
GLORIA
STEINE
GLORIA CONTINUED TO FOCUS ON SEX AND RACE INEQUALITIES ALONG WITH ABORTION RIGHTS, THE EQUAL RIGHTS AMENDMENT AND MUCH MORE. AS IF THAT WASN'T ENOUGH, GLORIA SOON BEGAN TO FOCUS ON THE ISSUE OF CHILD ABUSE.

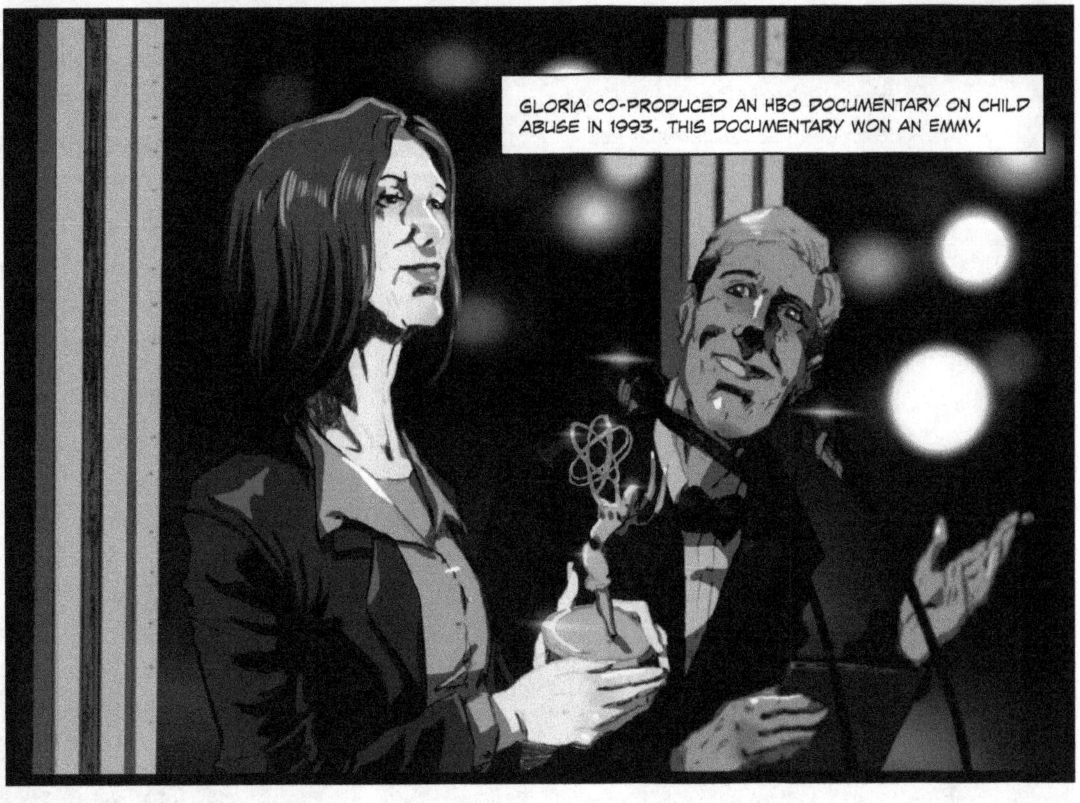
GLORIA CO-PRODUCED AN HBO DOCUMENTARY ON CHILD ABUSE IN 1993. THIS DOCUMENTARY WON AN EMMY.

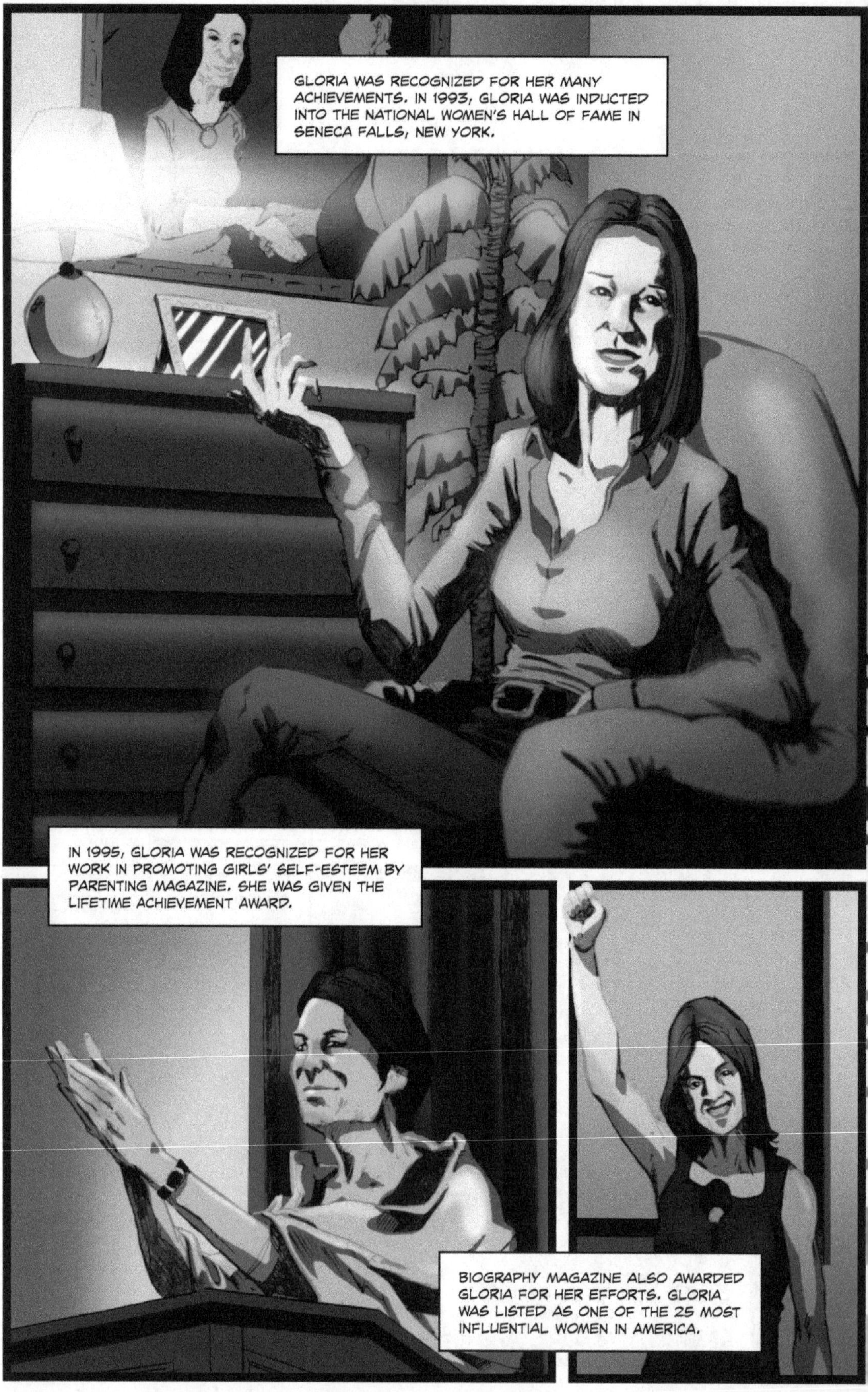
GLORIA WAS RECOGNIZED FOR HER MANY ACHIEVEMENTS. IN 1993, GLORIA WAS INDUCTED INTO THE NATIONAL WOMEN'S HALL OF FAME IN SENECA FALLS, NEW YORK.
IN 1995, GLORIA WAS RECOGNIZED FOR HER WORK IN PROMOTING GIRLS' SELF-ESTEEM BY PARENTING MAGAZINE. SHE WAS GIVEN THE LIFETIME ACHIEVEMENT AWARD.
BIOGRAPHY MAGAZINE ALSO AWARDED GLORIA FOR HER EFFORTS. GLORIA WAS LISTED AS ONE OF THE 25 MOST INFLUENTIAL WOMEN IN AMERICA.

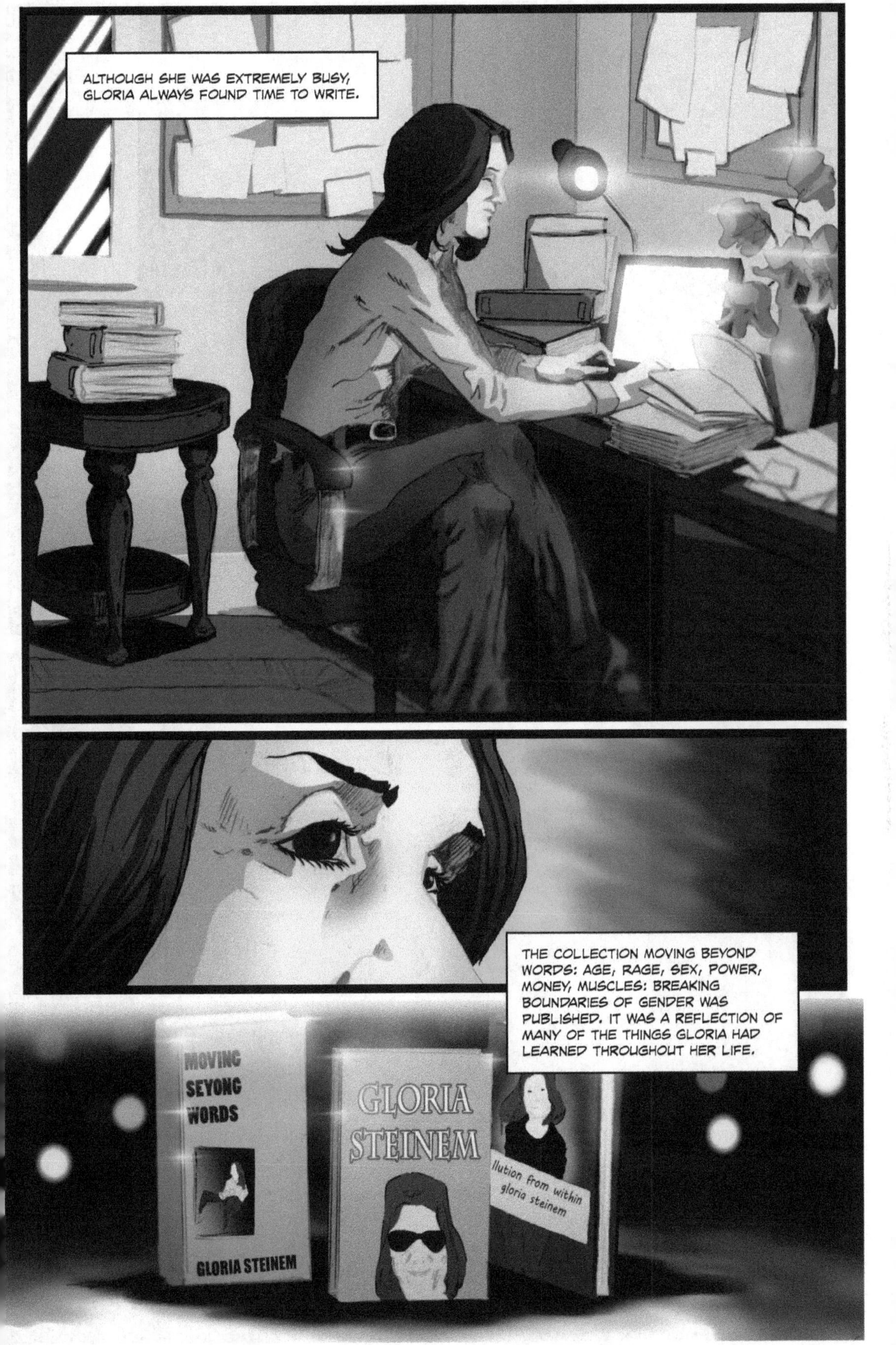

ALTHOUGH SHE WAS EXTREMELY BUSY, GLORIA ALWAYS FOUND TIME TO WRITE.
THE COLLECTION MOVING BEYOND WORDS: AGE, RAGE, SEX, POWER, MONEY, MUSCLES: BREAKING BOUNDARIES OF GENDER WAS PUBLISHED. IT WAS A REFLECTION OF MANY OF THE THINGS GLORIA HAD LEARNED THROUGHOUT HER LIFE.
MOVING SEYONG WORDS
GLORIA STEINEM
GLORIA STEINEM
llution from within gloria steinem

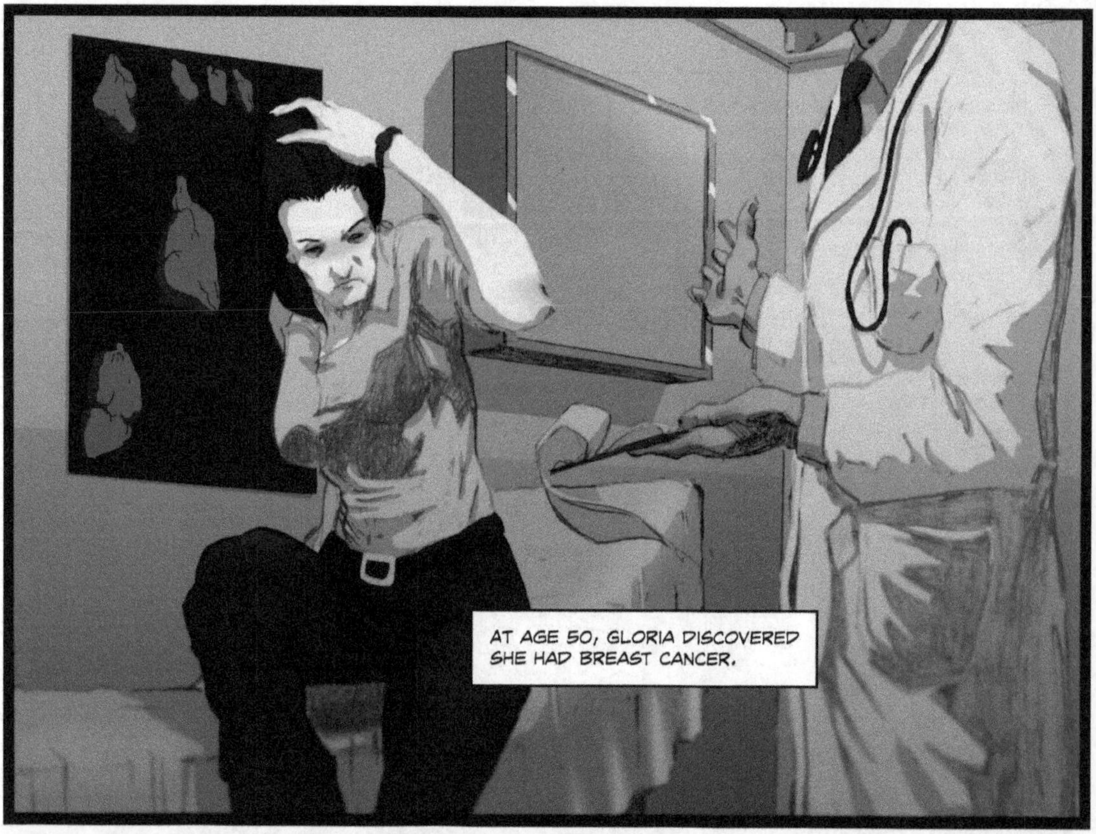
AT AGE 50, GLORIA DISCOVERED SHE HAD BREAST CANCER.

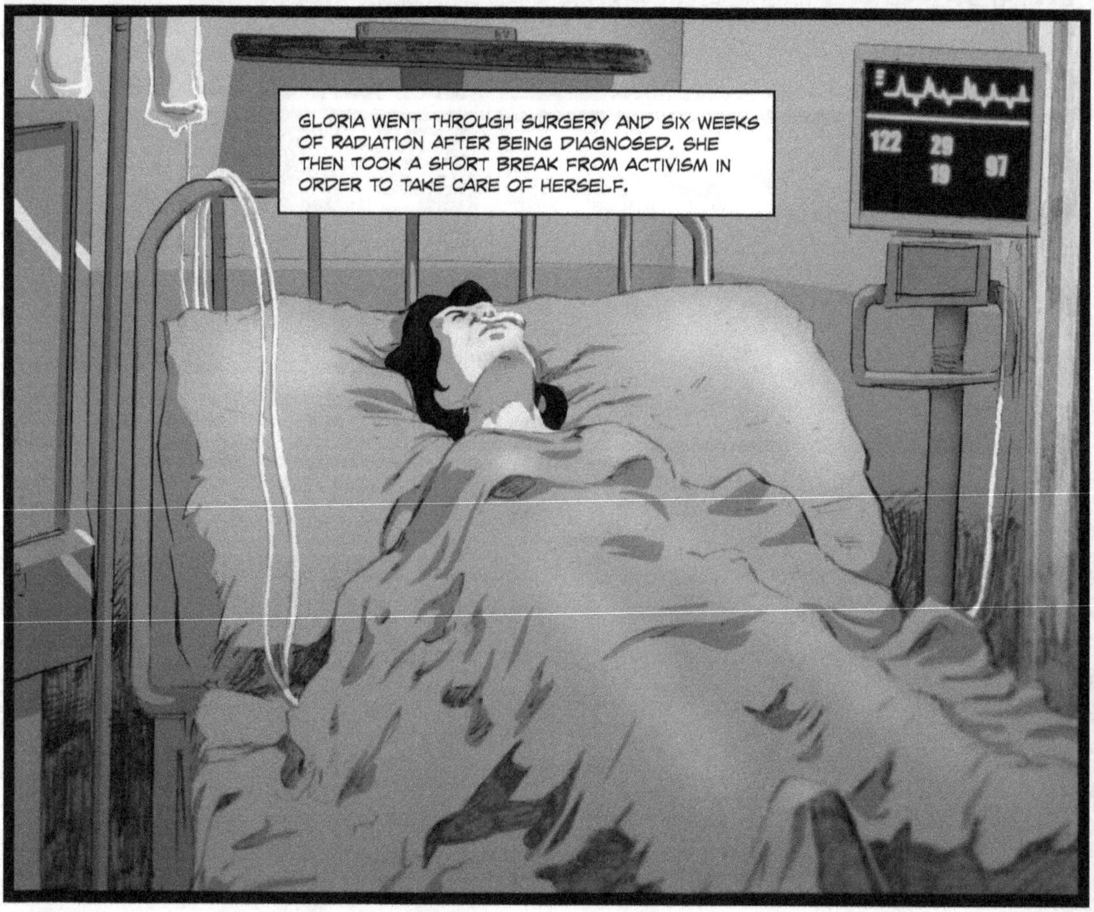
GLORIA WENT THROUGH SURGERY AND SIX WEEKS OF RADIATION AFTER BEING DIAGNOSED. SHE THEN TOOK A SHORT BREAK FROM ACTIVISM IN ORDER TO TAKE CARE OF HERSELF.
122 29 19 97

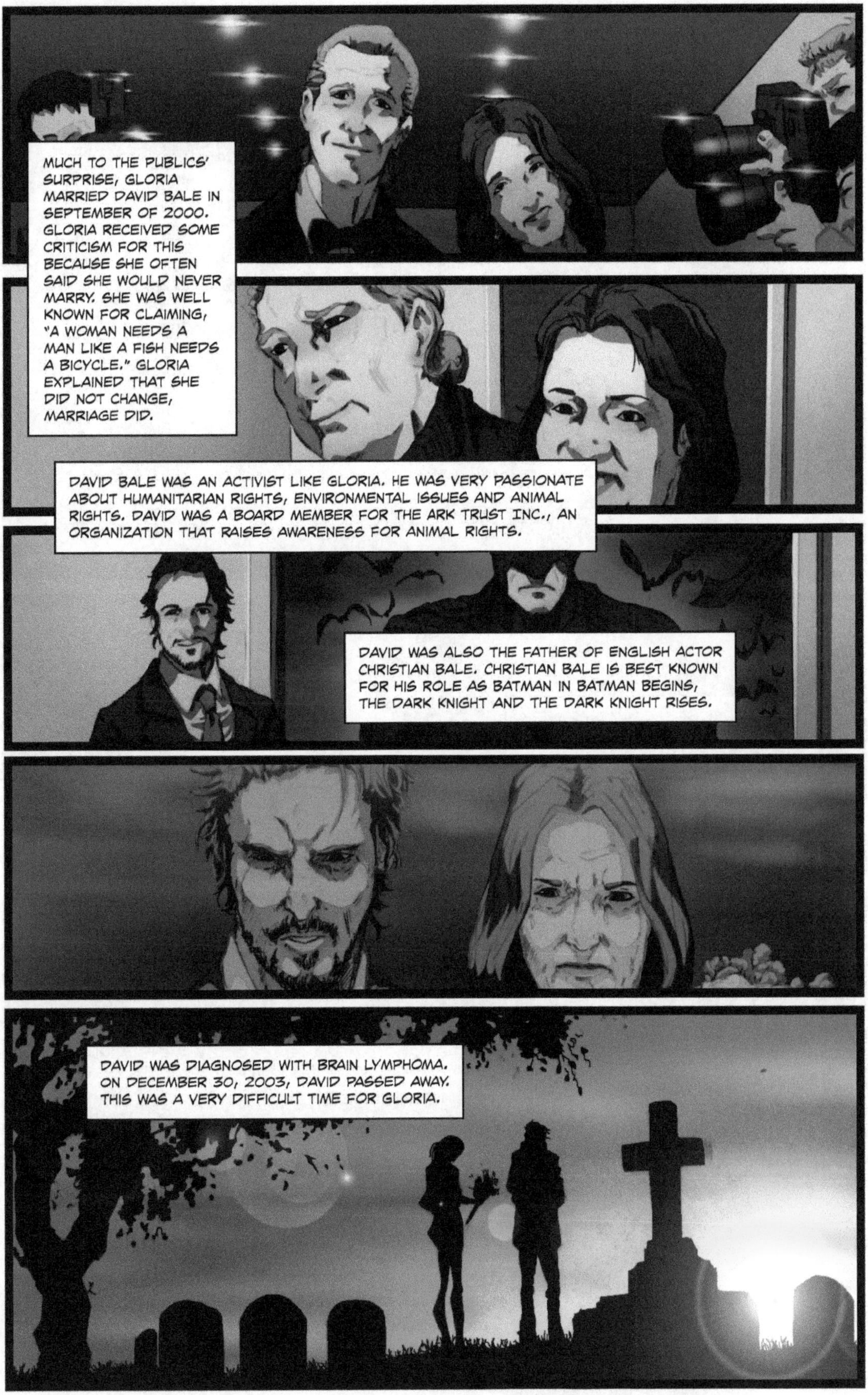
MUCH TO THE PUBLICS' SURPRISE, GLORIA MARRIED DAVID BALE IN SEPTEMBER OF 2000. GLORIA RECEIVED SOME CRITICISM FOR THIS BECAUSE SHE OFTEN SAID SHE WOULD NEVER MARRY. SHE WAS WELL KNOWN FOR CLAIMING, "A WOMAN NEEDS A MAN LIKE A FISH NEEDS A BICYCLE." GLORIA EXPLAINED THAT SHE DID NOT CHANGE, MARRIAGE DID.
DAVID BALE WAS AN ACTIVIST LIKE GLORIA. HE WAS VERY PASSIONATE ABOUT HUMANITARIAN RIGHTS, ENVIRONMENTAL ISSUES AND ANIMAL RIGHTS. DAVID WAS A BOARD MEMBER FOR THE ARK TRUST INC., AN ORGANIZATION THAT RAISES AWARENESS FOR ANIMAL RIGHTS.
DAVID WAS ALSO THE FATHER OF ENGLISH ACTOR CHRISTIAN BALE. CHRISTIAN BALE IS BEST KNOWN FOR HIS ROLE AS BATMAN IN BATMAN BEGINS, THE DARK KNIGHT AND THE DARK KNIGHT RISES.
DAVID WAS DIAGNOSED WITH BRAIN LYMPHOMA. ON DECEMBER 30, 2003, DAVID PASSED AWAY. THIS WAS A VERY DIFFICULT TIME FOR GLORIA.

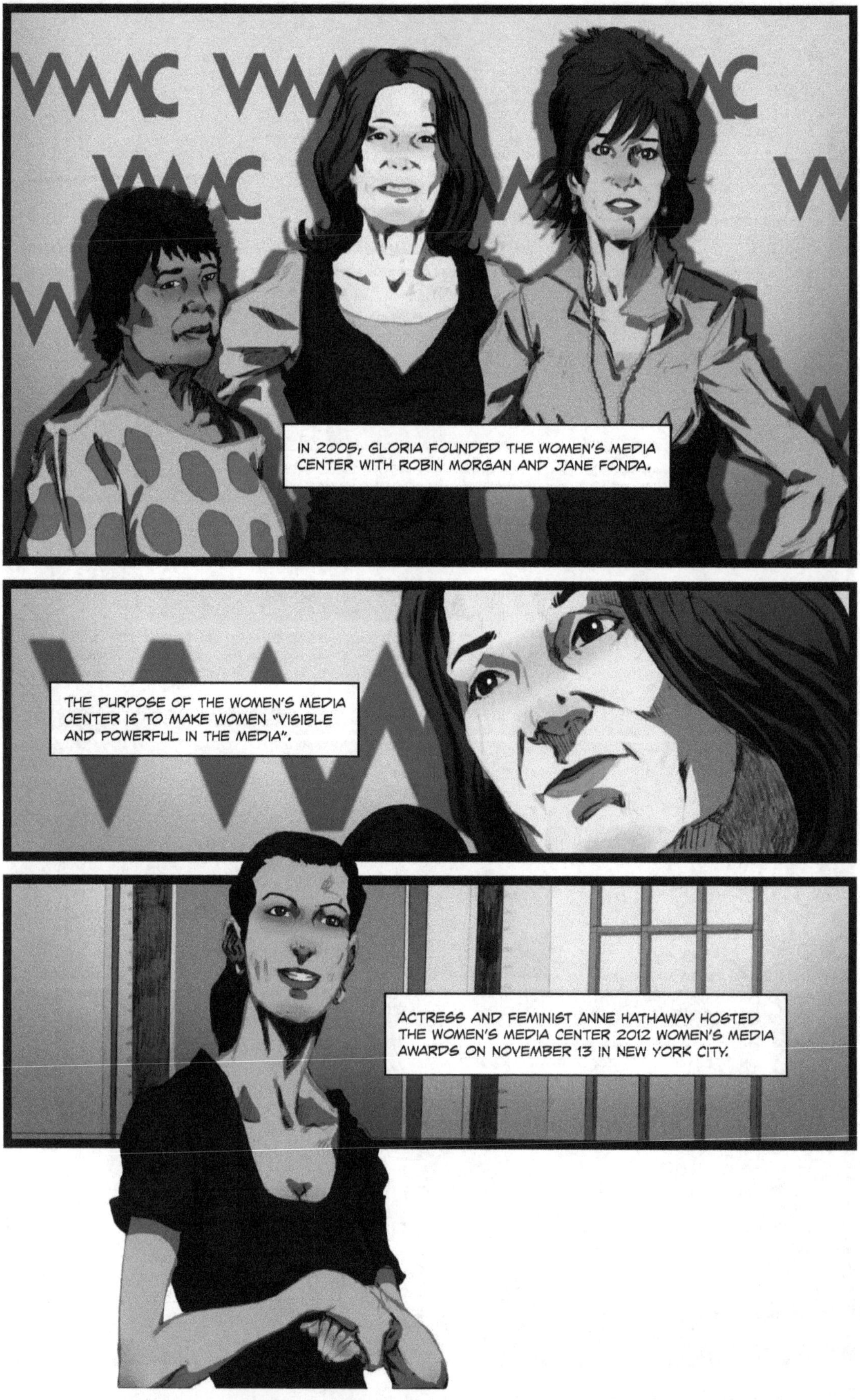
IN 2005, GLORIA FOUNDED THE WOMEN'S MEDIA CENTER WITH ROBIN MORGAN AND JANE FONDA.
THE PURPOSE OF THE WOMEN'S MEDIA CENTER IS TO MAKE WOMEN "VISIBLE AND POWERFUL IN THE MEDIA".
ACTRESS AND FEMINIST ANNE HATHAWAY HOSTED THE WOMEN'S MEDIA CENTER 2012 WOMEN'S MEDIA AWARDS ON NOVEMBER 13 IN NEW YORK CITY.

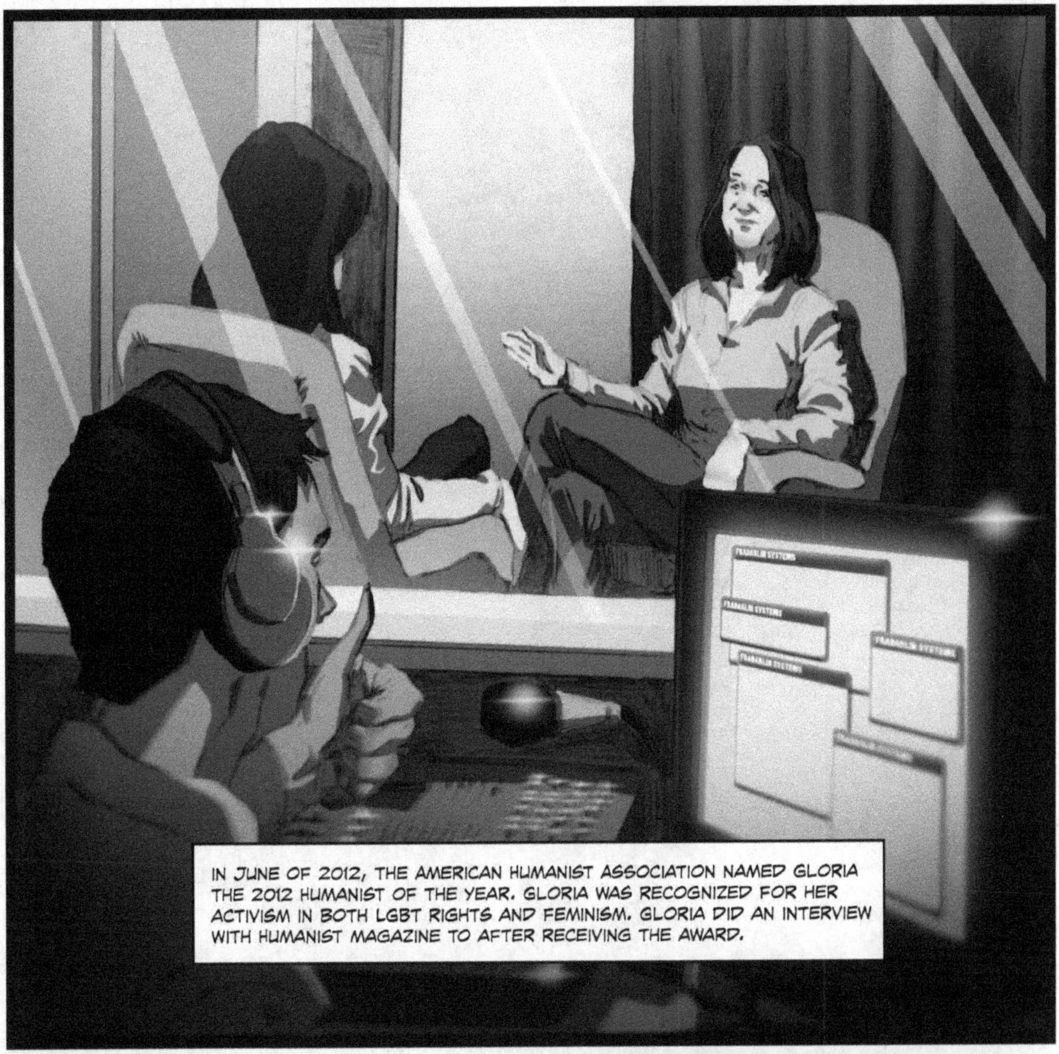
IN JUNE OF 2012, THE AMERICAN HUMANIST ASSOCIATION NAMED GLORIA THE 2012 HUMANIST OF THE YEAR. GLORIA WAS RECOGNIZED FOR HER ACTIVISM IN BOTH LGBT RIGHTS AND FEMINISM. GLORIA DID AN INTERVIEW WITH HUMANIST MAGAZINE TO AFTER RECEIVING THE AWARD.

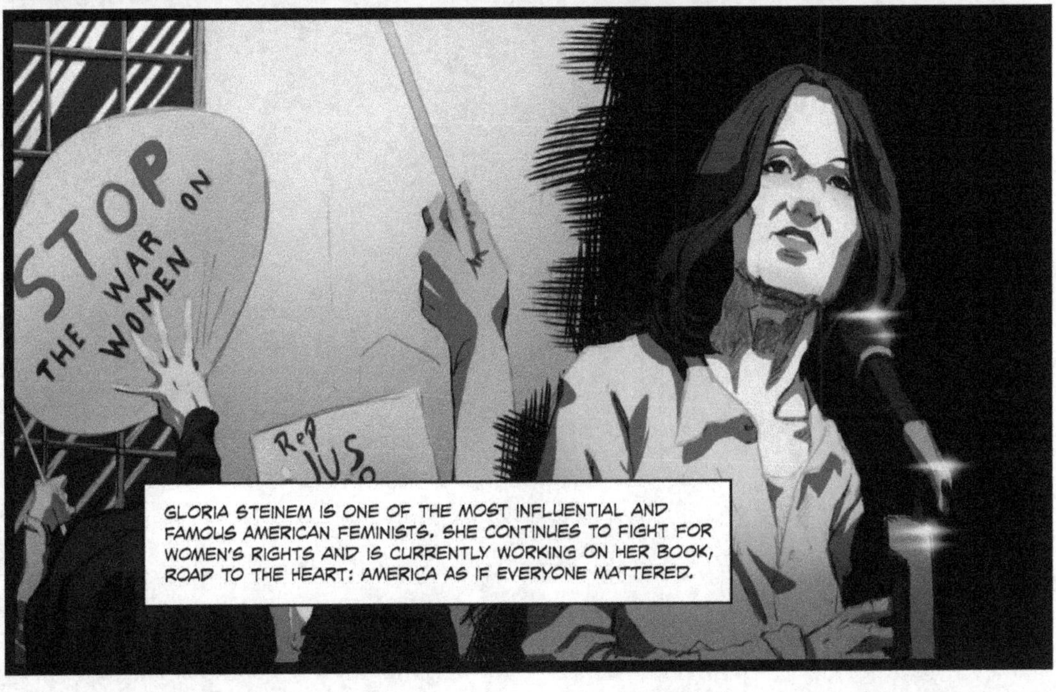
STOP THE WAR ON WOMEN
GLORIA STEINEM IS ONE OF THE MOST INFLUENTIAL AND FAMOUS AMERICAN FEMINISTS. SHE CONTINUES TO FIGHT FOR WOMEN'S RIGHTS AND IS CURRENTLY WORKING ON HER BOOK, ROAD TO THE HEART: AMERICA AS IF EVERYONE MATTERED.

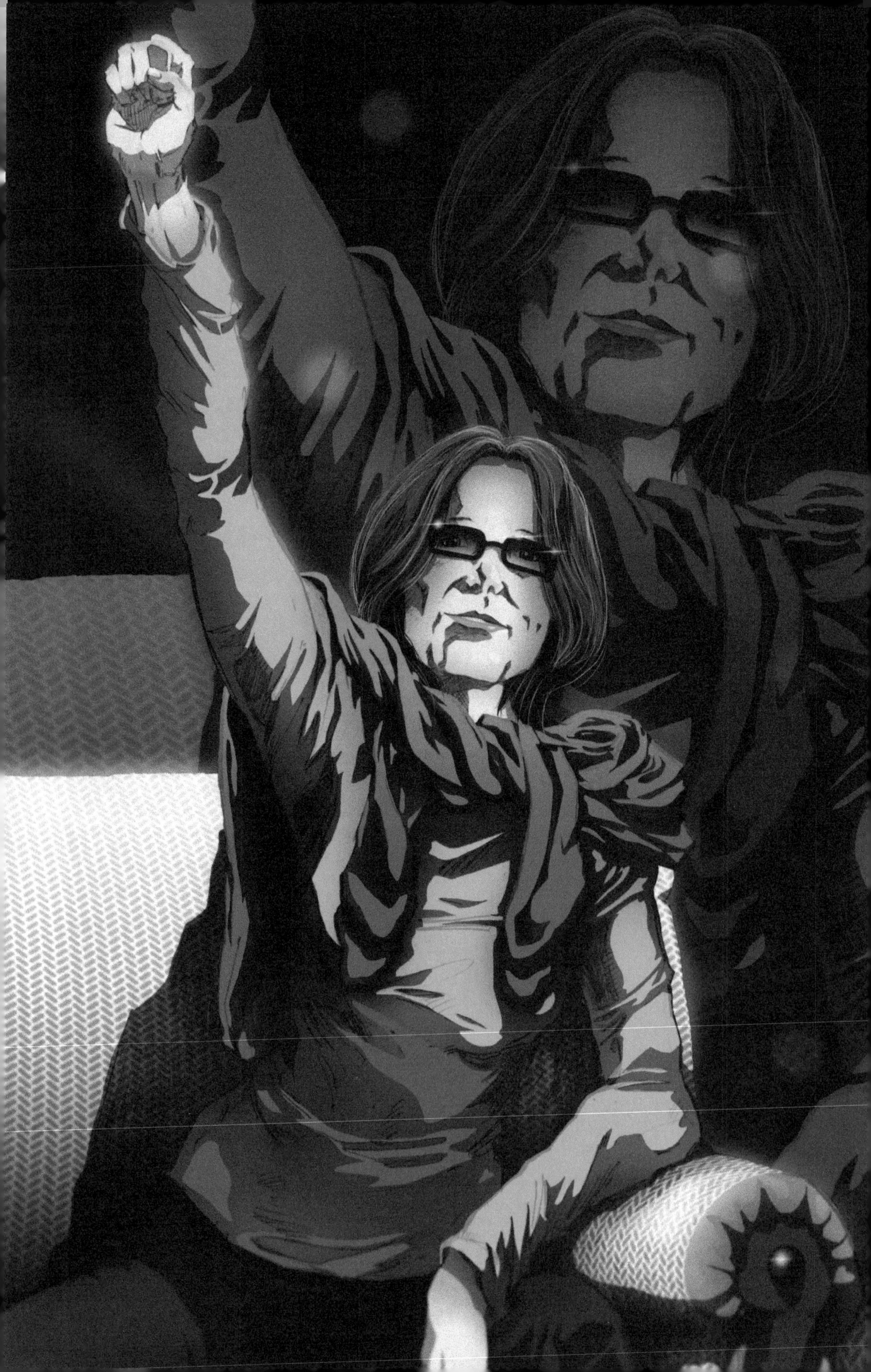

BLUEWATER COMICS

Melissa Seymour — Writer

Angel Bernuy — Penciler

Fradarlin — Colorist

David Hopkins — Letterer

Angel Bernuy — Cover

Darren G. Davis
Publisher

Jason Schultz
Vice President

Patrick Foster
Logo Design

Jarred Weisfeld
Literary Manager

Kailey Marsh
Entertainment Manager

Maggie Jessup
Publicity

BLUEWATER COMICS

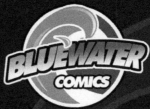

www.bluewaterprod.com

#ERASEHATE WITH THE MATTHEW SHEPARD FOUNDATION

With your donated dollars and volunteer hours, we work tirelessly to erase hate from every corner of America through our programs.

SPEAKING ENGAGEMENTS

Since Matt's death in 1998, Judy and Dennis have been determined to prevent others from similar tragedies. By sharing their story, they are able to carry on Matt's legacy.

HATE CRIMES REPORTING

Our work to improve reporting includes conducting trainings for law enforcement agencies, building relationships between community leaders and law enforcement, and developing policy reform in reporting practices.

LARAMIE PROJECT

MSF offers support to productions of The Laramie Project, which depicts the events leading up to and after Matt's murder. It remains one of the most performed plays in America.

MATTHEW'S PLACE

MatthewsPlace.com is a blog designed to provide young LGBTQ+ people with an outlet for their voices. From finance to health to love and dating, and everything in between, our writers contribute excellent material.

Erase Hate

Matthew Shepard Foundation
embracing diversity

CPSIA information can be obtained
at www.ICGtesting.com
Printed in the USA
LVHW060949110319
610189LV00012B/558/P